GHETTO BROTHER

How I Found Peace
in the South Bronx
Street Gang Wars

A MEMOIR

BENJY MELENDEZ

WITH AMIR SAID

Superchamp
Books SB

Brooklyn, NY

Published by Superchamp Books

Copyright © 2015 Amir Said

A Superchamp Books First Paperback Edition

All Rights Reserved.
No part of this book may be reproduced in any form by any electronic or mechanical means, including information storage and retrieval systems, without the expressed written permission of the publisher, except by a reviewer, who may quote brief passages in a review. Published by Superchamp Books, Inc. www.superchampbooks.com.

Superchamp Books™ is a trademark of Superchamp, Inc.

DESIGNED BY AMIR SAID

Cover, Design, and Layout by Amir Said

PHOTOGRAPHY
pp. 247-53, courtesy of Alejandro Olivera, Copyright © Alejandro Olivera
pp. 254-78, courtesy of Benjy Melendez, Copyright © Joe Conzo
p. 279, Copyright © Amir Said

Print History:
February 2015: First printing.
March 2017: Second printing.

Ghetto Brother: How I Found Peace in the South Bronx Street Gang Wars / by Benjy Melendez with Amir Said
1. Melendez, Benjy 2. Ghetto Brothers 3. Street Gangs of New York 4. New York History 5. South Bronx History 6. Hoe Avenue Peace Meeting 7. Memoir
I. Melendez, Benjy II. Title

Library of Congress Control Number: 2014958994
ISBN 978-0-9749704-6-2 (Paperback)

I dedicate this book
to Rita Fecher and Henry Chalfant

Part 1
The Village

Chapter 1
Little Boy

I was born in San Juan, Puerto Rico on August 3, 1952. It was interesting back then. At that time, most people were born at home. Same with me; I wasn't born in a hospital, I was born at home.

My mother already had two kids when she met my father, so I lived in San Juan at the time with my older brother and sister. My mother was very poor at that time. That's when my father first saw her. My mother said my father was always dressed nicely. When my mother and father first met, she said, "I always saw your father as an old man, very responsible, loves to work, very meticulous, very clean." And my mother was what my father always desired. "That's a house woman," he said. "And I wanted a house woman. I didn't want just a woman from the street."

My father always had money, and he would give my mother money for food for her and my older brother and sister. He'd say to my mother, "Get enough for you and your children." And my mother said, "This guy came at the right time."

One day, my father wrote my mother a note. My mother said that he told her that he wanted her to be the mother of his children. That's when he married her and took her out of poverty. He really loved her. He really cared for her. So he wanted to take her out of the condition that she was in. And that's what he did. So that's when I came into the picture.

At the time that I was born, Puerto Rico had become a commonwealth of the United States in 1952. The difference in age between my mother and father was way off. My father was born in 1900, my mother was born in 1923. *They were 23 years apart!* But my father looked good. As I got older and I looked at him, I would ask my mother, "Did Papi always look that old?" She would just say, "I met your father when he was an older man."

My mother was very skinny, beautiful face with black hair. She always had beautiful black hair. When she died, she was 75 years old — not one gray hair! It was all black. My wife said to her one time, "You colored your hair." My mother said, "Look at my roots, and you tell me if you find any gray there."

My mother was a very cool lady. She loved her children, we always really felt that. She took good care of us. She could do so much. She was good at embroidery, she was good at sewing, she was a handywoman, a housewife. She was GREAT at cooking. In fact, my mother used to make money cooking for other families.

My mother was short. My height comes from my father. They called him El Ruso, in Spanish it means "The Russian." People called him that because he was a big man. He was tall, with big hands. He used to go like this with his hands, "Get over here!" He was very imposing but kind looking at the same time.

My father was born in a small town outside of San Juan, in the countryside. I asked my father, "Papi, where was your father born? Was he born in Puerto Rico?" My father said, "No, my father came from Spain when he was 13 years old with his parents." So my grandfather came to

PR when he was 13 with his two parents. They were from northern Spain, Asturias. My father said they came from up there. He told me that his mother, my grandmother, was a half-breed. She was half-Indian and half-Spanish. She had hazel eyes. Tall woman with long black hair. One day, I asked my father, "Describe your father to me." And he goes like this, "You know Archie Bunker? That was my father!" I said, "Come on." He said, "No. He looks exactly like that."

We lived on Washington St. when I was a little boy, and we went upstairs to the second floor, which was my father's oldest sister's place, when we would walk in, it was like you're walking inside Spain. You know the women that wear those combs with the face going down, with the fans? That's what it was in those days. Remember, we were still very Spanish oriented, right. And then, you had the neighbors next door, Puerto Ricans. But everybody got along with each other. In the Puerto Rican society, this is black, this is white, but everybody is like this. So we all lived together. That's why when I went to the Bronx, it wasn't so much a shock seeing black brothers.

My father always acknowledged our African heritage, too. No doubt about it! See, in Puerto Rico, you have to understand something. There was a lot of mixture in Puerto Rico. In Puerto Rico, you're white and/or black. The Spaniards would keep the Africans in the coastal areas. When you go there, it's like walking to an African town. That's how black they are.

This was right next to San Juan. Any Puerto Rican could tell you. When you walk in, they have music called *la bomba*. Remember, like Aunt Jemima? They dress like that to this day. You know, the spiritualists? They do all that stuff. One day, I went back there, when I was older, and I'm looking at this black Puerto Rican girl. She was so BEAUTIFUL. I'm staring at her. There was an old black woman there, she says, "Ay, you! Don't look at her. She's got a boyfriend." Her boyfriend comes out. Brother — black, black, black. He said, in Spanish, "Hey, this is my lady." I said, "No, no. I understand." And my sister said, "Come over here." 'Cause in Puerto Rico, there is a little racism. But this is before the Americans. The Spanish already brought that in. But the Puerto Ricans, who are mixed people, embraced it during the course of the years.

After I was born, my father went ahead to New York during the Gran Migración (the Great Migration of Puerto Ricans). The Jones-Shafroth Act granted citizenship to the people of Puerto Rico. My father's sister already lived in Manhattan on 23rd Street. So when he went there, he got a job working for Consolidated Lumber. He was working over there, saved his money; eight months later, my father brought the whole family over. We moved to 420 West 23rd Street, between 9th and 10th Avenues. We lived in a community on 23rd Street that was beautiful. That area is still beautiful now, and it was beautiful then. Nothing's changed.

At that time, my family consisted of my father, my mother, my older brother, Bobby, my older sister, Candy, and myself. My brother Bobby was not much older than me. He was born in 1948, four years older than me. However, my sister was 10 years older than me. She was born in 1942.

My brother Bobby's real name was Ulpiano. He did NOT like that name. He said, "I hate that name, Ulpiano." So I'll give you the evolution of that name, Bobby. One day, we're all sitting around — my brother, my sister, and me — listening to music. There was an old song back in the day, it used to go like this, *"I wanna be Bobby's girl..."* So we were sitting there — this is when we lived on 789 Washington Street — and where we were sitting at is right where, as soon as you walk in through the door, there was a bedroom there. So I was there, and we had the phonograph, in the old days the 45s, right. We're all sitting around listening to this song, "Bobby's Girl," and we looked up, and my brother says, "You guys, from now on, don't call me Ulpiano. From now own, my name is Bobby!" I said, "I know why you want that name. Because of the song, 'Bobby's Girl.'" So from that day on, he became Bobby. And no longer Ulpiano. So we never called him Ulpiano again.

From 23rd Street, we moved to Harlem, up on 125th Street; the address was 3720. It was between La Salle and Broadway. When you see the train going down, that's where we lived, over there. Now during that period, I was a little boy, and the saddest thing happened.

My mother went downstairs for a few minutes to pick up the mail on the first floor. I was in the apartment playing with matches and I accidently started a fire. My mother had just finished coming out of the hospital; my little sister was just born, and she was asleep in the bedroom. I would play with fire, not knowing what I was doing or what could happen. I was only 5 years old. So, this one time, I was playing with fire and I threw it under the sofa, and the sofa caught on flames! My brother and I jumped on top of the bed. Before the flames had really started to rise, some people had come into the apartment and were trying to put the fire out. They ran back and forth to the bathroom; one took water from the toilet and tried to put it out, but the fire just kept growing. We were terrified.

The thing I remember most about that day is the fireman coming. He grabbed us. Took us down the hallway. I Looked and saw my mother screaming. And I looked, I was a child, staring at her, not realizing who was still in the apartment. My little baby sister died in the fire. She was just 2 months old. Her name was Luz. Luz Elenia Melendez. That was her name. I still have her picture in my head to this day.

Oh, my goodness! I felt terrible. It's something that has always stayed with me. The guilt has never gone away, even though I was just a little boy when it happened. My father was working at the time. They took her, my little baby sister, to Bellvue Hospital. Found out later on, the word *carbon* in Spanish means "charcoal." My father said she was "Crisp!" I remember he looked at my mother and said, "For one, two or three minutes you go downstairs and we lose a child?!"

But even before that happened, I didn't really know any better. I had a thing about heights. I would open up the window and step out on the ledge. My friends would always see me on the 5th floor, and I'm looking down. One time, there was a banana peel on the ledge of the window, and I sat on it. I was little boy, I didn't know any better. And there was an old man down on the street, yelling up at me, "GET INSIDE, GET INSIDE!" Just waving his arms like crazy for me to get back inside. Any moment I could've fallen down to the street. I would've been dead on impact. I almost fell, but nothing happened, though. And I just went inside. Don't tell me that that wasn't the hand of God. Because I should've been down there! Dead on the ground!

Then, there was this other dumb thing that I did. My hand is torn from here to here. My father had a giant fan in the living room. In those days, the fans were made out of metal, you know those kinds of fans? So, the fan was going so fast, I'm looking at it and I had a handkerchief and it went inside the fan. I stuck my hand in after it. BOSH!!!! And my hand completely opened up, blood everywhere. My uncle rushed me to the hospital. They sowed my hand back up. Shortly after that, is when everything happened with the fire.

I remember my father asking us about the fire. He said, "What happened?" Somebody had to tell. I said, "I didn't mean to do that. I was playing and I got burnt." And my father — very tolerant man, he loved all of us deeply — began to cry. You know, I was a little boy; I was his first son. My oldest brother is not from my father. So I was my father's first one. He had a big portrait of me in the living room, I remember looking at it before the fireman took us out. It got burned in the fire. I was just a little boy at the time. But the thing about it, when that happened and we got burned out of our apartment, we moved to Washington Street.

•••

Now we're at 789 Washington Street, in the Greenwich Village area. In that building, we lived in apartment 1R, right on the first floor. Our building was full of relatives, and my cousins lived on Horatio Street. There was one black family that lived in that building, too. I remember the girl, her name was Pepsi, and her brother, David. Now David, he grew up in our community, he spoke fluent Spanish. He was with us.

I went to P.S. 41. When I went to P.S. 41, the school was new, it had just recently opened. It was 1957, and I think the school opened in 1959. We were the only Hispanics in that school, and David the only black American, the only black dude in the whole school. We were the only ones from our community that went to that school.

Later on, I was told something that blew my mind. I personally didn't experience racial discrimination at that school when I went there, but one day, my sister tells me, "Benjy, when I went to P.S. 41, there was a certain teacher, I never forgot her. When I was watching Channel 13 the other day, I just saw her. And you know what she said to my class when I went to P.S. 41? She said, 'Everybody with dark eyes and brown eyes sit in the back, and people with blue eyes and green eyes sit in the front.'" Crazy.

So between Washington Street and Horatio Street, it was mainly relatives. Cousins, aunts, extended family. We all lived in the same area, family and friends, you know. But we were surrounded by the Irish on Hudson Street and the Italians on 10th Street. In that Washington Street community, all the people were very close. The families were tight! You could feel the love. You could feel the atmosphere, the festivity in the air. People looked after one another. "I'm gonna tell Juan" (that's my father's name), someone would say if they saw me doing something wrong. I'd be like, "Aw, man." So everybody, if they see us on the block doing something wrong, they would be like, "What are you doing around here? I'm gonna tell your father."

My father was a man of character. He didn't play! We were expected to be a certain way. Everywhere we went with my mother and father, we knew to behave. My mother told my wife now, Wanda, that "All families loved our children. Because our children would go into somebody's house and they would sit in the sofa. They would not move from there unless their father gave them permission."

And it's true. We would play with those kids and their toys, and after we finished we would help them put the toys back and come back and sit down. When you're at the table, you could talk. But don't make a scene. 'Cause if my father looked at you, that's it! He had a habit that the belt always got in the way. And you know what I mean. My father was not having it! You knew you had to behave around him. If we were playing in the street, as soon as he put his head out the window and we looked up, we'd be like, "Uh, guys, we gotta go." Him looking out the window meant that we had to go upstairs. So we'd go upstairs, take a bath, get ready for bed, say our prayers, and get ready for school for the following day.

My father said he wanted us to have a strong work ethic. "Papi, can you give us money?" We'd ask him, and he'd say, "You want money? I got four buildings here. I want them swept, I want them clean. And then you come to me. You're not gonna get money for doing nothing. You're gonna work for it." He taught us those things. And his thing was his name. The name Don Juan, you heard of it right? Don in Spanish is like, Sir John. So, Don Juan is equivalent to a Sir, like in the English, Sir John or Don Juan. So whenever anybody said these words, *Don Juan*, it sent shivers up all of my family's spine, because we knew, once that man hears it, we shamed him, we did something that we should have NEVER done. That's the way my father was. He didn't have to hit you, he just *looked* at you.

And everywhere we'd go, I learned. When he was talking to his friends, I would be like this, looking at him. 'Cause I loved the conversation. My father looked to the side and he knew I was watching him closely and listening. "Let him hear it, it's O.K," he'd say. As long as it wasn't something very private, he would let me stay and listen to him and his friends talk. I was looking at these men, observing. I saw my father's actions, the way he spoke, his gestures.

My father was constantly reading the Bible. That's what encouraged me to get into it even more. Every Friday night, he would gather up my family. We would go into the living room and then he would start chanting. So, I looked forward to it every Friday. We'd be in the living room and I was all ears. I just wanted to listen to what he said. And he made stories beautiful. My earliest memories of our Friday nights was when I was 7 years old. My father was always teaching us about the Bible. We were Catholics — on the outside, you know, to everyone else. And some days, we'd go to church. But we were really a

Jewish family, Catholic on the outside because we had to be secretive. On Friday nights, my father would gather all of his children. We would be playing outside. So he would say, "Come inside." My father would sit down, and we're all sitting down in the living room. He'd pull down the shades, close the door, real secretive. And then we'd start talking about the Bible. Specifically, his main hero was always the prophet Moses. He was teaching us knowledge. It wasn't until we got older that we realized that he was really teaching us Torah! And that it was Shabbat.

So we'd go to church, and I'd ask "Well, why do we do it?" And my father would say, "You gotta do it." So you know, we had to do all of this, we had to go to church, but we weren't Catholics. We had to hide who we were. At church, I kept on looking at the statues. "Worship statues?" I'd say to myself. "We don't do that!" Then, my father would say, "Be quiet."

I remember we'd walk around Delancey Street, on the Lower East Side, and he'd say to me in Spanish, "See, the Jews don't work on the Sabbath." And I said, "Then, how come we don't do that?" He put his hand over my mouth. That's what he did to me. So we'd go to church on Sundays. That was the big thing. Go to church on Sunday like everybody else in the community, to hide who we really were. We weren't living in Spain, we weren't living in the Inquisition days; but that trauma was still there. That trauma from the time of the 1400s up until now had been past down from generation to generation. The fear! The fear that if you tell people that you're a Jew, that's it. My father feared telling people that we were Jewish. So we had to be secretive about it. At the time, I was young.

I didn't really understand why we were one way at home, but had to be another way out in the community. But I knew we were different from the other Puerto Ricans in the community.

Either way, everything was better in that community, especially for a little boy. When it was Halloween, THAT was Halloween! When it was Thanksgiving, IT was THANKSGIVING! All the holidays, all the love, the unity of the families. It's not like you see it today. I mean, in those days, your parents bought you suits and you would have to wear a shirt and a tie. And you go to worship. And you're constantly looking at everything; I was always looking at my father, observing everything that he did.

I remember we'd come out of school, my cousins and I, and then we'd go to a bakery store called Bon Bons, it was on Jane Street. And we used to say, "Any Bons, any bons?" you know, just being kids, playing around, harassing them. The man from Bon Bons would come and we'd run. He'd yell, "Get outta here!" Finally, one day the people from Bon Bons came and gave us free cakes and pies. I took eight of them. We took them around the block and gave them to our parents. Great time.

Then there was an incident. One day, I had a sandwich in my hand; I was gonna give it to my friend Rocky. We were little, like The Little Rascals. So I was on my way to give Rocky the sandwich. As soon as I hit the corner of Jane Street, I turned to my left and I saw a horrible sight: A truck drove by and crushed Rocky! He was just a little boy. He was looking down into a manhole when a refrigerator truck drove by and crushed him from the toes to the front. I remember seeing his little brain being squashed out. It was a terrible thing to see even for an adult, but I was just a little boy. To see that right in front me like that? We all started to cry. I still had his sandwich in my hand. I said, "Aw, man, NO!" And I never seen so much blood. That image is still so vivid in my mind today.

Even now, I go there and remember Rocky. I took a picture of the manhole and I told my children, "My little friend died right here." They said, "Papi, you still remember that?" Of course I still remember that! How are you ever going to forget something like that, you know? After Rocky died, all of the parents were like, "Get inside the house!" All of the parents were looking out for the little children because we were their life.

That community that I used to live in was nothing like how Greenwich Village is now. In those days, they would bring you milk, your milk was delivered. Every morning the milk man would put the milk out in front in the morning. It was a glass bottle of milk. In the old days, they even had a horse and buggy. The guy would come around selling pots and pans. He was an old man; and people would go out into the street to buy pots and pans from the old horse and buggy. The streets were cobblestones. It was not the way you see now, you know, the tar. It was cobblestones.

Across the street was an old train, you know what they're doing with the Hudson River? That train that they're making into a park? Well, that train, that's the train that ran to where I used to live. Every morning we would get up and go to school, and we would look at this train, the old locomotive train. It was a black locomotive thing, pulling all these cars. If you go there now, aw, it's beautiful! Whenever I'm back in that neighborhood, I stop people and I say, "Did you know, I used to live around here?" And then people look at me like I'm crazy and say, "Oh, what do you mean?" It's all white people there now. So they're like, "What do you mean?" I tell them, "Yes! My uncle lived right here. My sister lived up there." I say, "Did you know there used to be a bar over here?"

And while Greenwich Village is different today, you know, all different types of people; I didn't know nothing about gays back then. My brother used to say, "In the basement." There was this place where they hung out in the basement. Because it was closed, nobody knew about that. Remember, the gays were behind closed doors in those days. There was also a nice grocery store. I tell people that I stop on the street in Greenwich Village, "Did you know there used to be a grocery store over here? And there was a grocery store right over there on the corner?" Again, they look at me like I'm crazy.

Oh, man, the grocery store was beautiful. I bought a soda — a Veep soda — a sandwich, and a cake for 35 cents! The store was beautiful. The wood, shellac wood. And the name of the owner was Stevie. They were Albanians. Nice people. Everybody liked them. And they were serving the Hispanic community there. Around the corner was another family that lived up there, another grocery store.

At that time, most people lived and worked in or around the same area. There was a meat area. My father worked at Consolidated Lumber, which wasn't too far away on 23rd Street. Walking distance or take a quick bus ride. Knowing my father, he'd walk over there.

Music was big then, too. So the people in the area had bands there. My uncle was one of them, we used to call him "*Tío* Tony," Uncle Tony. He was a band leader, he ran a band, an orchestra. They used to play on the 3rd floor, in the Washington Street area. So we used to listen to all of this type of music back in the days.

My uncle was also known for being a doctor when it came to birds. So on the train station, you know in the train right under the train station where the birds lay eggs? So we used to get the eggs and bring them to him. He'd take care of them and they'd hatch. Or if a bird was hurt, he'd take care of it.

•••

It was on Washington Street in Greenwich Village where I first became like a leader with some guys. We used to hustle spare change, opening cab doors and stuff. That was our business, that's how we used to work. So I said to all the little boys around the block, "All right, let's do it!" I was 7 years old, but even then I was operating like a leader, getting the kids to cooperate. Look how we cooperated as children, "All right, look guys, this is how it works. We're gonna go straight down the road. The minute you see a light, you say *Mío*! In Spanish that means "mine." Mío! That means, all the kids get out of the way, I open the car door, and they give us money. That's how we accumulated money. Night, day time. Whenever.

There was a bar on Washington Street between Horatio Street and Jane Street. That's how we made our money. The best time to make money was on Halloween. Or sometimes when we were desperate, we would just ask somebody for money, "Oh, Sir, can you give us a quarter?" And one time, this man gave me a dollar and I went insane. Because in those days, a dollar was worth a lot! A hundred pennies? You could buy a hundred pieces of candy for a dollar.

It was also in Greenwich Village that I had my first understanding of turf. And in those days, the sad thing about it was, we lived like a real *West Side Story*, you know, the movie. You had the Irish, the Italians, and the Puerto Ricans. Each group had their area. There were a lot of Puerto Rican and other Hispanic families living in Greenwich Village at that time. But mainly they lived on Washington Street.

My older brother, Bobby, would say to us, "Be careful going up to Hudson Park. Don't go over there." That was where the Irish guys hung out, that was their turf. But my brother Bobby could go over there because the Irish guys liked him. Now, why did the Irish guys like my brother? Why did the Italian guys like my brother? Because he's got blue eyes and curly blond hair. He *looked* like a white boy. He used to say, "This is my little brother." So they didn't do nothing to me 'cause Bobby was my brother.

They'd say to my brother, "What are you doing over here, when you should be with us?" And my brother would be like, "Oh, these are my boys over here." But my brother Bobby was never a fighter. Bobby was known for running fast, and he was a good swimmer. But Bobby, I never seen this guy getting into an altercation. He's a very cheerful guy. He gets along with everyone. So when you ask him, "What nationality are you?" He says, "Yo, I'm a man of the world." That was him: *"I'm a man of the world!* Everybody's my friend." So that's Bobby for you. Everybody liked my brother Bobby.

You couldn't go to Hudson Park because that's Bobby Gallagher's boys — that's his turf. The Irishman, Bobby Gallagher, he was the leader of a gang of Irish kids. So one day I was with my cousin Joe. And we looked across the street and we see Kayo, one of my boys, screaming and jumping. Bobby Gallagher had hit him with some barbed wire, right around the legs! I never forgot that. So Kayo's running towards us, we run back to the block. We knew that Bobby Gallagher's boys were not going to come down here.

That was the very first time that I started to organize some guys for a fight. As time went on, I became more influential with the young kids on the block. I said to my cousins and my friends, "Why don't we get together and defend ourselves against Bobby and his boys if they come here?" We were little, and here I am talking about how we had to defend ourselves. I said, "We gotta defend ourselves against these guys over here."

Our turf was Washington Street, all the way to the river. Their turf was from Hudson up. So we couldn't go over there. If we were with the older guys, we could go with them. So, I had a plan. The bikes in those days had these old, big baskets for putting groceries in. So one day, I look at my brother and say, "How many people could you put in there?" He says, "Two or three." So I'm thinking of a landing craft, stuff I seen on television. I told two or three guys, "Go into their turf and just throw rocks at them." The thing is, even at this time I was already thinking of war strategies. 'Cause I was thinking military.

One day, we got into an altercation, and Bobby Gallagher's boys were on Hudson Street and Greenwich Street. We were on Horatio Street, coming up from the other way. I told my boys, "Go around the corner and let's get them!" And we did it. We got them right there. We surrounded them. WE PELTED these guys with rocks. I felt like I had accomplished something major. That was because I was thinking. I said, "We can't let these guys get away with what they did to Kayto."

When I looked at my brothers and the guys, and I saw the movie *West Side Story*, I said, "There they go!" That was Bobby Gallagher and his boys and the Italians. That's the way they looked back in the days. You know, all the guys over here. Italians over there. We were in that small community, surrounded with all these people.

In those days, you had the cops with the long jackets. You've seen those pictures. The cops used to be like, "All right, move along!" They were all Irish. You had to be in the middle of the block. You could not be on the corner. "Get in the middle!" they would say. Since my friend Rocky was killed, crushed by a truck, they wanted everybody in the middle of the block. "You can't hang around there. And, stay away from 10th Street," the cops would always say. They were talking about the older guys, my brother and his boys. "Stay away from 10th Street. And leave Bobby Gallagher and the guys alone. Leave those guys alone," the cops would say. When you say Bobby Gallagher, EVERYBODY knew who he was.

• • •

We left Washington Street in 1963. All of the Puerto Ricans were now starting to migrate to the Bronx. It was about the money. The landlords in the Village were selling the apartments. They were giving people money to move out, to *move out*! Money was coming in, development and stuff, and they wanted us — the Puerto Ricans and other Spanish families — out. They were transforming the place.

When I went back, years later with my brothers and friends, I saw how everything looked, the development and the people, and I thought to myself, *That's why they wanted us to move*. I walked up to a person and said, "Excuse me. Do you have an elevator in there?" "Yeah," they said. When I lived there, we never had an elevator in there. Another thing I said to the guy on the street, "The stairs are made out of porcelain." And the guy says to me, "That's the way they were." "No, sir," I told him. "Our stairs were made out of wood." It was all wood. They got rid of everybody, all of the Puerto Ricans, then completely modernized the place. The rent now in that area is extravagant.

As a little boy, I didn't really know everything that was going on, you know. I didn't know why we were being pushed out of our homes, out of our community. I just knew that all of the families were moving to the Bronx. Older people in the community always believed that the surrounding communities and real estate developers didn't want us there. They wanted those buildings and they wanted the land. They didn't want the Puerto Ricans, though. They wanted our particular community to move out. So the landlords gave some people money to move out. Remember, in those days, people were strapped for money. Others, they just pushed out. So, the landlords were like, "Here you go! You want this money?" All of the landlords were going like that. The last Spanish families that stood there was my cousins; but then, even they migrated to the Bronx.

We all said, "Why did we move to the Bronx?" Another reason was because most of the Puerto Rican businesses were going there. The Jews moved out of the South Bronx and Puerto Ricans started to move in. And when Co-Op City was built later on, people started to move out of there.

We were one of the many Puerto Rican families that moved to the Bronx. My father went to explore the South Bronx. He had friends and family already there. So he said, "Here's were we're gonna go, because most of our friends and people are moving in this area. I want to be in an area where I know people. I don't want to go over here and then start exploring. Who's this and who's that?"

So when we moved to the Bronx, it was 1963, right after the death of John F. Kennedy. I remember the day John F. Kennedy died. I was in school at P.S. 41. I was standing on a line outside of class. All of sudden, I started seeing teachers crying. I asked, "What happened?" "The President was assassinated!" it came through the loud speakers.

I went home and when I got there I saw my parents crying. I said, "What happened?" You have to understand, Kennedy was a hero to the Puerto Rican people. People had Kennedy rugs and pictures in their houses. EVERY Puerto Rican family that I knew back in the days had

Kennedy something in the house. Kennedy was the big guy in those days. When he died, it was like, "Aw, man… That was our President, man. He was looking out for the poor."

Right after that, my father started to pack up. He said, "All right, listen. I got a job up there in the Bronx. I'm taking us out of here. 'Cause everybody's over there. We're not going to stay in this building here." The landlords, we knew, later on after I became a Ghetto Brother, they just wanted these buildings to renovate them. So all of the Puerto Ricans were pushed out and ended up moving to the Bronx.

Part 2
Culture Shock

Chapter 2
The Junior Beatles

When we first moved to the Bronx, we lived at 789 Stebbins Avenue, between 163rd Street and 164th Street. It was my father, my mother, my older sister, Candy, my brother Bobby, me, my younger brothers, Victor and Robert, and my younger sister Judy. We were right across the street from Junior High School 133. Victor, Robert, and I didn't go to 133, 'cause we were still kids. We went to P.S. 23.

I experienced culture shock when we moved to the Bronx. It was an entirely different scene. When we moved there, I said, "What is this? This is not Manhattan!" 'Cause we were used to something much different. Life in Manhattan was more calm. Over here, it was a different world. My brother and I started to explore the area. My younger brothers, Victor and Robert, always had a tendency of being together. I was always alone. I just wanted to be alone. So we started to explore the area.

I went up to Prospect Ave. I went around there and was like, *Oh, this is fantastic!* There were four movie theaters — the Vernon theater, the RKO, the Loews, and the Parson on the corner. I said to myself, *This is BEAUTIFUL! Look at this!* I remember the movies we first saw there. We saw three movies — *Hard Day's Night*, *Hercules Unchained*, and a James Bond 007 movie. 50 cents! The movies were 50 cents in those days.

So we explored the area, places, businesses. We saw a lot of businesses, bustling houses. A lot of families. Big community of people. A lot of black and Puerto Rican people lived there. We lived in a real community, you know. You had the blacks that lived on Union Avenue and the Puerto Ricans that lived on this side.

I remember when I went to P.S. 23 for the first time. My hair was combed back like I was a guy from *West Side Story*. The first time I went to the class, what did I see? It was all blacks! It was only me and this guy Louie; that's it; he and I were the only Puerto Ricans. The rest were all blacks. And I had an incident, a little fight with this girl, she was black. My father couldn't make it to the school 'cause he was doing business; my mother was sick. So my oldest brother represented my parents. He comes to the school, says, "What happened?" I was a young boy at the time. You know what she said, the girl? She said, "I didn't start it. It was this *white boy*." She called me a white boy! I didn't say, "Don't call me that." 'Cause I didn't know who she was talking about. I was Puerto Rican, I wasn't white. I was a little boy. I said, "I didn't do that. I didn't do that." So they left it at that; neither of us got into trouble.

After that incident, after a while, like all newcomers, we started getting along. So I sat with Louie and people thought that we were brothers. That's when I started to experience racism. Now remember, in the Puerto Rican community, discrimination? No. We got Puerto Ricans of different colors. So to us, it was no new thing. But remember, we were exposed to a lot of American stuff now. Whereas on 23rd Street and 14th Street and 125th Street, it was a Spanish world to us. You understand what

I'm saying? So when we first moved into the Bronx, I felt alienated. I couldn't talk Spanish around here. So we had to learn English.

We learned English from our friends outside. 'Cause in the house, my parents only spoke Spanish. We also learned English by watching all the television. My hero in those days was John Wayne. I used to look at John Wayne and say to myself, *I want to be like him.* 'Cause he was a Marine. In those days, there were a lot of war pictures. I was amazed by John Wayne and the war pictures. I would imagine being a leader of a whole bunch of guys, and they're all listening to me.

It wasn't too long before I started making friends at P.S. 23. After I made friends with Louie, I made friends with a guy named Tommy, he was a black kid. Tommy was cool. Little by little, it just started to naturally work itself out. Then I met a guy named Reuben, then a guy named Willie Vasquez. That's when I started to get to know people around the community.

This was also around the same time, early '64, I met my friend Raymond Gonzalez. Raymond lived in the last building on the block. But there was something wrong with his moms. He used to live in the streets. I felt bad for him, so we became friends. I told my father about him. I said, "Pa, he lives in the street. Can he live with us?" And my father said, "This is not an orphanage." So you know what we did? My brothers and I? We snuck Raymond in the back door. One day, my father comes in our room, looks at him in the bed, then turns around and walks out. From then on, my father never said anything. Raymond became like one of us. He grew up with us in the family.

My father took him in and he became like a brother to us.

This was also during the time that I first discovered The Beatles. We're sitting in the apartment and my brother walks in and says, "Hey, guys! There's these four faggots;" remember, in those days you didn't say gays. So my brother says, "There's these four faggots coming from England. They're called The Beatles." "The Beatles?" I said. "Yeah. They're going to come down here." It was my brother Bobby, he introduced me to The Beatles.

Raymond and I went to Prospect Avenue and Westchester Avenue and we saw the jukebox in his uncle's restaurant. In those days, they used to put the sleeves in the jukebox. And what do we see there? The Beatles. We were like, "THERE THEY GO! Those are the guys!" I said, "Oh, look at them!" Raymond said, "Look, they got long hair!" When you think about it, though, they really didn't have long hair, compared to *long* hair. Raymond was like, "Aw, man, they look funny with their hair like that." So we put the coin in the jukebox. First song, "I Wanna Hold Your Hand." Aw, man, my hair stood up! I was like, "Aw, they're so cool!" We fell in love with these guys.

After that, we went to this old newspaper stand right there on Prospect and Westchester. The old newspaper stands used to sell magazines with the songs of the groups. A lot of bands back then had their songs in magazines. We bought *The Beatles Manual* and we looked it over and saw all the songs and pictures, then we went and bought their first album.

I remember when The Beatles went on the Ed Sullivan Show. We were all glued to the television. We were all excited, everybody's screaming, "Aw, man, they sound cool!" After that, we started practicing their songs. You know where we learned to sing harmony from? Alvin and the Chipmunks!

We didn't know how to play the guitar at that time. So Raymond bought a snare and a cymbal. And we just clapped our hands. We knew all of The Beatles songs. We'd go out into the streets and play live. We were called The Junior Beatles! It was five of us — Raymond, Victor, Robert, Justino, and me.

The girls used to chase after us; it felt like the movie, The Beatles movie *A Hard Day's Night*. Aw, man, it was like The Beatles. We're running down the block, all the girls would surround us. Sometimes we'd be inside on the couch singing and they were all there. It was a nice time.

Once, we were playing this one song, and these two guys, I remember one of them, his name was Caesar, the other guy I forgot; they were dressed in suits, and Caesar says, "Young men." We looked up and said, "Yes." He said, "We're looking for a group called The Junior Beatles." And I said, "That's us!" He takes out a yellow ticket and says, "Tito Puente knows who you are, and you guys are going to open up for him." I said, "YOU SERIOUS?!"

So the first official place we played was the Embassy Ballroom. I remember when we where announced, the guy says, "Ladies and Gentlemen," in Spanish, "Los Junior Beatles!" Now, I had a harmonica. Tito Puente's over there. We're singing and the crowd is roaring. And remember, the only instruments we were playing at that time were the drums, the cymbal, and a harmonica. When we finished, the people went insane.

Around the block, there was this one guy named Theo, a black brother. And every time Theo heard us play the song "This Boy," he would cry. It was a Beatles song. So you know what he does? He would call us from my father's house and yell, "Hey, Junior Beatles! Hey guys! Can you sing me that song?" It's a three/four harmony song. Listen to the song, it goes, *"That boy took my love away, and he'll regret one day/Cuz this boy wants you back again."* Theo said, "He's talking 'bout me in that song, man. You know why that reminds me of me? Because it reminds me of the guy that took my girl." So every time we sang that song, Theo would just start crying. So this one day, we go out on the ledge of the building — where we lived on the second floor — and we started to sing for him. Then we had a little crowd. And Theo just couldn't stop crying.

The next place Tito Puente's people got us involved in was the Colgate Gardens. We played Colgate Gardens, and after that we played American Legion, then we played the Tropicana. I was 12 years old when all of this was going on. We remained the Junior Beatles until John Lennon said his famous quote, "We are more popular than Jesus?" Once he made that statement, we didn't want to be with it anymore, 'cause we were a very religious family. So we became The Junior Rolling Stones. It was for a little while, but we didn't like their songs. Then the Monkeys came out, so we became The Junior Monkeys. And after The Monkeys, we came back to The Junior Beatles when we heard *Abbey Road*. Then, as years went by, the songs were waning. We already had celebrity status in the community as The Junior Beatles. So we decided to just keep the name.

Those were innocent years for me. I was a happy person. Right next to the soap box, my father's room was right here, there was a record player. We had The Beatles. Crosby, Stills, and Nash. Alvin and The Chipmunks. The Supremes. Sly and The Family Stone — I really liked them, very revolutionary to me. James Brown. Aretha Franklin. Lots of really good music. Stuff that had a really big influence on me. So I would stay home in those days, and all I did was listen to music.

Later on, in the Ghetto Brothers, when I got full of music and my belly was full from eating my mother's food, I went to the block. You see what I'm saying? When the guys saw me happy, they were happy. And it was very rare for me to use bad language; profanity was never in my language. And if I did use it, all the Ghetto Brothers knew me for this, it was rare. But they'd say, "If Benjy starts using profanity, get ready, he's gonna start swinging!" I had a raspy voice, so I intimidated people when I spoke. But I also made a lot of people happy. So these were my innocent years, before the Ghetto Brothers. But then later on, that's when everything started to change. That's when the buildings started to come down.

• • •

In 1963, I started a gang for the first time. It wasn't really a *gang* gang, you know. This was way before the Ghetto Brothers. I had The Barbarians and the Hell Riders, on Prospect Avenue between 163rd Street and 165th Street. These were two different clubs altogether. The Barbarians — we wore masks, like the wrestlers. If you couldn't afford the mask, then you waited to Halloween;

then you buy the mask. It was like, at least 15, 20 of us; nice kids, we were just having a good time. But it was just like a precursor.

The spot where I started the Ghetto Brothers was on Marmion Avenue and Tremont Avenue. That's also where I was once a member of the Cofon Cats, where Kool Herc — DJ Kool Herc — was a member. I never knew what the meaning of the name was. I remember some of the guys from the Cofon Cats. It was Craig, Willie, Kayto, who became Huey, my friend. And Herc was there. He was probably there earlier, because when I joined that club, he was gone. I was told that Herc was in that gang. But when I got there, I didn't see him.

But yeah, I started the Barbarians way before the Ghetto Brothers. It was in 1963, I was 11 years old. I stood with the Barbarians for a time, until my father caught me up on the roof. He gave me the whooping of my life! He said, "What are you doing?" I said, "Pop, these are my friends." But it's fear. It's not the fact that I was with my friends in a little gang. It was the fact that I was on the roof! In those days, young people were not supposed to be on the roof. And it was an abandoned building. I could have fallen or something. My father gave me a beating in front of all of my boys. What could I do? I loved him, you know, I respected him.

What made him come up to the roof was the fact that some people in the community were tight; everybody knew each other. If you were doing something you weren't supposed to be, they'd tell your parents. So they were like, "Hey, Don Juan. Your son is up there." My father was probably like, "Oh, yea?!" Man, when I saw that big shadow and I saw that belt, I knew it was my pops. I was terrified. But there was nothing I could do, I had to take the whooping.

We weren't doing anything crazy up there. I was just getting the guys together, setting up rocks, "O.K., guys, let's put all of the rocks over here and the bottles in case we get attacked." *Nobody attacked us*. It was imaginary. We were looking at the backyard. I saw Junior High School 133. We were pretending that people were coming at us, we would just throw things.

Down below, people were like, "Hey, your son is throwing rocks over there!" When my father came up to the roof, oh, my goodness. He gave me the whooping of my life, I was terrified. He was a big man. Then he tried to grab me. So I ran down the stairs. And he said, in Spanish, "I have you sentenced!" *I had to go home eventually*.

When I made it home, I went to my refuge: my mother. "Mommy, please. Please, don't let Papi…" My father came in right after me. He said to my mother, "You know what he was doing up there? He was throwing rocks." "Yeah, but he wasn't throwing it at the crowd," my mother said, trying to defend me. "He was throwing it at the yard."

I told my father I was sorry and he grounded me. He had me clean the house. I had to sweep. The house had to be constantly clean. My mother and father always had this thing about a clean house; and they were alwasys watching out for their children. Every time they would look out there, they wanna know exactly where we were. If you were on the corner, you gotta be on the corner. If you're playing handball, you have to be there at the hand ball court.

In this same year, in the middle of all of this stuff with the Barbarians, I started the Hell Riders. Some of the members were Piano, Willie, Speedy, Robert, David, Boar, Franky, and me. These are the names I still remember. We were just a bicycle club at first, you know, we were just having good times. Our flag was the old Mobile gas station flag. The Mobile gas stations used to have these flags. When we did the Hell Riders logo, we all had bicycles; everybody had bicycles. So our flag, we went to the gas station and we took the flag, the Mobile flag with the red horse and the wings. So everywhere we'd ride, that thing was with me. 163rd Street. Kelly. Fox Street. Tiffany. That was all inspiration. When young people saw all these guys with bicycles, what did that do? They wanted to be part of the crowd.

At that time, it was like 20, 25 of us. The Hell Riders! Think: 25 young kids with BICYCLES! And I did that strategically because I knew that it would encourage other young people to say, "Yo, man! Can I join your club?" And I'd say, "Yeah. But you have to have a bike! You gotta get a bike, my brother." That's the only thing you had to do to get in the club. You had to have a bike. Nothing like the initiation you had to go through to get into the Ghetto Brothers later on. The Hell Riders was just a fun thing. And what if somebody wanted to jump us? They couldn't attack us. Why? Look, there was way too many of us! That was our idea. It was after my time in the Hell Riders and the Cofon Cats that I started the Savage Nomads on Freeman Street.

During this time, it wasn't bad yet. People were into stickball, playing basketball in the parks. Generally at the time, people were happy, having fun, getting along. The buildings were still up. People were still respectful and having a good time. Playing dominos. Kids were into sports, oh, especially football, basketball, and baseball. Everybody was into that. Our thing, the Hell Riders, was just riding around.

And where did I get the idea for the Hell Riders from? I got that idea from the Hell's Angels. I saw magazines, guys with chopped-down motorcycles. Some of the guys in the Hell Riders had chopped down bicycles. I couldn't afford to do it. But, you know, we looked majestic going down the block. And the people saw us and were like, "Oh, there goes the Hell Riders!" And when we came down the block, all these bicycles, and I'm looking at the kids and you see they're like, "Ohhh!!!"

We had Maroon bikes, the old Maroon bikes. Some of us had chopped-down bikes. 10 speeds. The 10-speeds, the 21s. Those and Maroon bikes. Even the 3-wheelers. And, man, that inspired kids to come up the block saying, "Ay, who's the President?" The guys would say, "Benjy." Then you'd hear, "Benjy, can I join?" "Yeah, do you have a bike?" "Nah." "But you gotta get a bike. How can you ride with us if you ain't got a bike?" So, the gangs in the past, they would have to steal a bike. We didn't do that. No, huh-uh. You had to buy one, or maybe talk to one of these guys here and see if they have a bike to sell you. But that was fun in those days. Nothing crazy or really *gang* like going on.

Then after the Hell Riders, I was in the Cofon Cats. The reason I left the Cofon Cats was because I didn't want to be under nobody's leadership. Because then, that man, I would have to do what he says. I'd be under his rule. But the Cofon Cats were cool. They were a gang who took care of their community. They were very central. Their main nemesis, our main nemesis, were The Reapers. They were in the Bronx Zoo area. Guys were BAD dudes! Their colors were beautiful. Now, in those days, the gangs used to paint their colors on the jacket — paint them. Some of them had satin jackets with the letters on it. I saw that and I said to myself, *Man, they paint the colors on the jacket?!* O.K., fine. So, I left there. Then I started a new gang. And that's around the time when things really started to change in the Bronx.

Chapter 3
When the Buildings Started Coming Down

The buildings started coming down in early '68, '69. The Bronx was changing from what it was in 1964, just after my family first moved there. There were riots on Third Avenue. If you went to Third Avenue in those days, before the buildings came down, you could see everything. There were no gates. You could walk to Third Avenue and see everything. My first time walking on Third Avenue I was like, *Oh, this is nice!* It was like Manhattan to me, like where we used to live. But when the buildings started coming down, aw, man, things changed.

It started to get dirty. The beauty of the Bronx was gone. People started throwing garbage cans in the middle of the street. And all of a sudden, there's widespread discrimination, lack of employment, bad housing, you know, no jobs. Nothing! There was no money, people had nothing or next to nothing. So this caused a lot of anger, a lot of frustration.

But there's one thing I noticed that really stood out: the blackout! When the riots were going on, and I was looking at the television, and my father says, "Here's what makes it worse!" He was talking about the general condition of the Bronx. My father knew how bad things were in the Bronx. I think he saw the change coming. This was between '68 and '69. I specifically remember seeing the moon that night, it was beautiful. But the riot was going on. My brother stayed inside the house. It was that bad. On the news, you saw people breaking in stores and shops, taking out televisions and things like that. Even as a young boy, I knew that was wrong. I was like, *Why are they doing that? Why are they stealing this?* It's one thing to show your anger. But it's another to take that anger and do mischief. I thought to myself, *Wait, What about that guy who owns that store?* That could've been me, that could've been my father.

After that, they started putting the gates on stores and shops. And then when everything was calm and started building back up, little by little, I looked and I felt sad, I was like, *Man, I can't see that anymore; can't go in there anymore.* I remember this store, Florsheim. We would stand at the glass and look in. We could always walk inside and see everything. After the riot, the man who ran the store said, "No, you can't go inside." Things like that were changing. Now, everywhere in the South Bronx people didn't feel safe. People started to move out. The businesses started to pack up and go. Those who could were leaving fast. All of the white people, they were leaving. Gone!

There were a number of things that caused all of this. One big reason was city management. The city took over many of the apartments and they didn't do anything about them. The landlords at that time — everybody was talking. "The landlords!" my father said. "You know that guy over there? They're no good." Most landlords were hiring people to burn the buildings to collect the insurance off of them. The landlords didn't care. They were making money. They couldn't care less about the people in the community. Same with City Hall.

When we first moved to the Bronx on Stebbins Avenue, after the death of President Kennedy, everything was good. We moved from our apartment on Stebbins Avenue to 789 Tiffany Street. From '68 to '70, we lived at 953 Fox Street. It was a beautiful five-room apartment. We lived in apartment 8. Everything was going good in that building. Each floor had two apartments; that's how spacious and big it was. It was nice. Heat, everything. All of sudden, the city took it over. I said, "What happened?" My father said, "Management." There used to be management, the landlord. He'd collect the rent, take care of the place, make sure the upkeep always happened. Then all of sudden, he was GONE!

Next thing you know, people started stealing water pipes from our building and the surrounding buildings. There was no hot water. My father was desperate. People were moving out. My father said, "No, no. I can't do this. I can't live like this." So, he went out looking for an apartment. There was no apartments available because people were moving and buildings were burning. The buildings were coming down! This started ratcheting up in '69, and that's when the gangs, little by little, started to spring up. Anger and frustration was boiling up and spilling over.

I also remember the Cross Bronx Expressway. It was mostly already built by this time. And the damage had already been done by Robert Moses and them. Older people used to tell me, "You know, there used to be houses there." I was like, "Say what?" "Yes! They took 'em all out." They just destroyed them to make way for the Cross Bronx Expressway. They took everything out! The biggest slumlord of them all, ROBERT MOSES! "How you gonna get rid of this?" *Take everything out!* that was his solution. *Just take everything out!* You know what I mean? But where are the people going to go, where are the poor people going to live?

Even as a kid I knew about Robert Moses. We were there in the schools and in the community, you had people who taught you things. There was one guy who talked about it in our community. I forgot his name. He was an older black man. And he said, "See what Robert Moses did?" And I'm saying to myself, *Who's Robert Moses?* "Yeah, this man is tearing up this whole place. And a lot of people are moving out. Where's those poor people gonna go to?" Everybody knew about Robert Moses, but it was this black guy who first put me on to him. My goodness, instead of getting a place for all of the people who were forced out to make way for the Cross Bronx Expressway, Moses just knocked everything down. In other words, he was like, *You're on your own!*

So I'm hearing this, and my brothers and I went to explore the area. And we see blocks — that used to be full of life — just plain gutted and burned out. Where are these people? Moving on to other places in the Bronx. Now remember in those days, you had to have money to move up to the north Bronx or out to Long Island or Queens, where the whites from the Bronx moved to. So people were desperate to keep an apartment.

Like I said, people stole the pipes from the building that we lived in during this time. So here's what my father did. Around the corner, there's this group of abandoned buildings. He saw a building, saw that it was locked with a chain. He broke it. He went to the first apartment; it was warm. Nobody lived in the building. He took our family there. He paid guys from the street to help us move. We lived there for one month. BUT, we had hot water! Nobody lived in the building except for us.

We lived there for one month. Now remember, I was always outside. You know, I always took it for granted that my father would take care of everything. A month later, we moved across the street from 153rd Street to 94 Tiffany. That's when my father found an apartment on the top floor. And it was a beautiful apartment — as beautiful as you can get at that time. After living in an abandoned building, it was like moving to a penthouse. We lived there from 1970 to 1975. And during that time, the Bronx was lousy! Nobody should've been forced to live in such conditions.

Put it this way, there was this movie *Wolfen*? When they did the movie *Wolfen*, we were looking at this, and I told this guy working there, "Look at this. They have a natural setting." They didn't do it in Hollywood. They did it right here in the South Bronx, where the buildings were all messed up. Abandoned buildings, just burnt out shells where homes used to be. They did it in a natural setting. If you ever see that movie *Wolfen*, and you see the area, that was the South Bronx at the time. That wasn't no Hollywood set that was designed to look like a disaster. The South Bronx was a real disaster!

And I looked at this, you know, and said to myself, *That's really sad*. And then, when I saw the whole area like that, my brother was talking to me. My older brother, Bobby, went to Vietnam. When he came home, I said to him, "You know, Bobby, it's really bad over here, man."

He said, "Benjy, Vietnam was bad!" "It's bad news over here, too," I said. He says to me, "What you talking about, man? I lived in Germany after the war. So what are you talkin' about?" "Yo, Bobby, you see, you got killings over there on a larger scale. We got the same thing over here. You said you seen dead people? We see 'em over here, too. All the time. All right! But we're on our home ground! And this is its own war zone."

Some people try to put the blame on the people living in the buildings. You know, they tried to blame the fires on the residents, not the landlords or the fire department. The fire department didn't always do what they were supposed to. And the city closed down a lot of firehouses. And some people want to blame the residents for that? NO! That's not true, it wasn't the residents' fault. You can't blame the residents for all of that. The residents didn't create the situation or the conditions.

Aw, man, back in the days, a lot of times the landlords, some of these landlords were paying people from the street — usually junkies, drug addicts, and even some gang members. They would pay these people to do arson, to burn the buildings so they could get insurance. The city KNEW this was going on. The city KNEW what was happening in the Bronx, they just didn't care. It was terrible. The buildings were coming down everywhere. Entire lots, blocks just burned out. Some people, I remember a friend of mine saying, "You know, Benjy, I have to sleep with my shoes on in case there's a fire, so I can run out." I said, "You serious?" "Yeah, man…" That's how crazy it was. Fires were happening everywhere, and you had to be on alert all the time.

Around my area, we were looking out for our building, making sure that nobody went around burning up the building. So between Prospect and 162nd Street and Stebbins Avenue, we were always looking out. The main fires were usually on Tiffany Street, Fox Street, all those areas. Later on, when I was a Ghetto Brother, around the Ghetto Brothers turf, where we were, there was hardly ever a fire around there. And if there were fires, they were like four or five blocks down, 165th Street and up. We would walk up to the junkies, "Yo, yo, come here, guys. Don't be doing this, man. They're gonna pay you guys money to burn our buildings." They'd be like, "Nah, we ain't gonna do that, man. That's not what we're about." Yeah, right, we knew what the deal was. And I also know that there were gang members from other clubs that were being paid off to do crazy things like that.

The burning buildings was widespread. It was a big problem! I mean, the South Bronx looked like World War II, like Germany after World War II. When you walked down the street — especially around Freeman, Tiffany, and Fox — and you looked up, the only thing you saw was a beautiful moon on a summer night. Nothing but empty shells of empty buildings. If you didn't know, you'd think the Bronx was a war-torn area. That's what it looked like, like a bunch of tanks just blasted buildings up.

It was a really sad sight because when I moved to the Bronx, after the death of Kennedy, it was beautiful! The Bronx was beautiful, you hear me? You had stores, you had beautiful buildings, banks, bakeries, you had beautiful places. There was no fear. People walked around freely. The community was together. The buildings looked beautiful, they were clean and well kept. People had their homes. Families were together. But when the buildings started coming down, I saw the deterioration, little by little. The distortion of the government, of the Mayor's office. They didn't wanna do NOTHING in our community. It's like they said, *You know what? The hell with you people*, you know, *Have a nice day. We'll take care of Manhattan. We'll take care of 5th Avenue and Park Avenue. You people kill yourself up there.* That's the impression we got from these people in City Hall. That's how they treated the people of the South Bronx.

And one of the worst things about the buildings and the fires is how it was burning families right out of their homes. It was a sad case. It's like, you had parents and people who would take their family to their churches. And here you got parents and working people. Where are we going to move to? Where are we gonna live? The whole place surrounding us is being burned down! And we can't go uptown, the rent is too expensive. We can't move up there. You couldn't move to the north Bronx, they don't want us to move up there. Where are we gonna go to? We can't go to Long Island. Nobody had any money, and the social services the city provided were being decreased in the South Bronx during this time. Man, it was a disaster on lots of levels.

The burning buildings, the gutting of the Bronx and all of that, that played a huge role in the emergence of the gangs. You had families being split up all over the Bronx. Relatives had to find a place to stay wherever they could. If a relative had room to take someone in, fine. But even then, it would be overcrowded. So mothers, fathers, brothers, sons, daughters — families were just split up. This destroyed the togetherness that the community used to have when we first moved to the Bronx. People had no where to go. It started being about nothing but survival. So the gangs started to come up, much more violent and sinister. And all of the kids who were in the kid clubs, the childhood gangs, we all started to become outlaws.

Part 3
The Deathtrap

Chapter 4
Becoming an Outlaw

In 1967, I started the Ghetto Brothers on Marmion Avenue and 180th Street in the South Bronx. I was still a Cofon Cats member, and Kool Herc, the godfather of hip hop, was there around the time that I joined. But I don't remember seeing him. Years later when he spoke about his background, he said he was a Cofon Cat. I said, "Hey, Herc, I was a member of the Cofon Cats." It must've been when I came in he already left.

Actually, before I started the Ghetto Brothers, I was in a couple of other gangs. The Cofon Cats and such. I got into the Cofon Cats for protection. But I got tired of being under somebody else. I said, "Guys, I don't wanna do this anymore. I wanna start my own thing." So I left the Cofon Cats and I went back to Marmion Avenue, right across the street from where the Cofon Cats were. I took a leather jacket, I put it down, and I started to paint for the first time: GHETTO BROTHERS!

Originally, the colors were white and green. It was, you know, the Lee jackets. So we painted the whole back of the jacket white. Waited until it dried, then we added the colors inside, so it could look nice. I put "Ghetto..." The background was white. And it was just "Ghetto Brothers," the letters, no insignia, nothing yet, right in the middle.

When I did the colors, and I said, "Look!" and I showed my girlfriend, Maylin, who later became my wife. She helped me put it together. She was a good artist. Designer, really creative. So Maylin said, "Yeah, that looks good."

I started to wear the jacket. I was a one-man gang. Walking around, alone, with my jacket. Then little by little, I went to my old block. The old guys from The Barbarians, the old guys from The Hell Riders, they saw this and was like, "Yo, Benjy…" The guys were like, "Yo, Benjy, what's that, man? Is that your new thing?" 'Cause they knew me by that, always starting something new. So I'm like, "Yeah, yeah! This is gonna be my new club, Ghetto Brothers! You wanna join?" They said, "Yeah, let's go!" Now, it's five guys who wanna join. To do those colors for five guys, you gotta paint five jackets. Dry. You have to paint everything.

Then, one day I went to see that movie *Hell's Angels on Wheels*, and I saw the Hell's Angels, you know, the Hell's Angels motorcycle club. I saw the Hell's Angels' colors, and I said, "Yo, maaan!" I told my brother — Ghetto Brother — Ulpiano, "Look, Piano, look! Check that out, man. Look, look at the colors, it's made out of material." So I caught the idea for how to do the Ghetto Brothers jackets — with the colors and the material — from watching that movie.

So we went to the fabric store. Up on Webster Avenue, there was a material store. So we bought felt. I took a piece of hard cardboard and I cut out rockers. I put it on the felt, I traced it, then I cut the rockers. Then I went to Harry's Sports Store, which is not there anymore, on Southern Boulevard between 163rd Street and Simpson. Every gang — after what I did — started to go there. So we bought the letters. Old English letters. "GHETTO BROTHERS!" Then we put it on the felt. First, it was this way, "Ghetto Brothers New York." Later on we changed it to just "Ghetto Brothers." To me, "Ghetto Brothers New York," looked better though.

And when we did this, then we ironed on the letters. After we ironed them on, we went to the cleaners. The cleaners is still there, but it's closed. The spot is still there. We gave those people jobs. They were working a lot. The cleaners made money, big time, doing colors for all of the clubs. You'd go in and they'd say, "What do you want?" "I want you to take this. See, look, it's ironed. Sew on the jacket and sew each letter so it won't come off, 'cause we ironed them on." So they were getting paid, 'cause it was a lot of Ghetto Brothers and all the other gangs, too.

Then, I wanted to know, what kind of patch I should put in the middle. We took the patch, then we did our own painting. The original painting was a skull and fire with the Puerto Rican flag in the middle. Then I said, I can't do that 'cause the flag looked like it was buried, so I took it off. And besides, I had members that were not Puerto Rican, there were other nationalities that were in the gang. So we took that off. I drew a skull and then I drew fire. Now, where did I see this before? Same thing, but with wings? Hell's Angels! It looked like the same thing. That was part of my inspiration. I did "Ghetto Brothers New York," white, with red. Hell's Angels was white and red. You gotta ask their permission, 'cause that's their colors. And, oh, man, did I find out!

Here's what happened. One day, my brother Victor, along with Charlie and Joey, go to West 4th Street in the Village. The Ghetto Brothers at this time are much bigger, meaner than when I first started. This was 1970, several years after I first started the Ghetto Brothers, right. So, you know when you look in the window at the merchandise and you see the reflection of somebody behind you? Somebody says to them, "Hey, YO! What the hell is that?! Take those things off!" Victor, Charlie, and Joey turned around, and who's standing there? Some Hell's Angels! "Get it off!" the big guy yells to them. Then the Hell's Angels took their colors off of them!

Now, I was already gaining a reputation. If any gang wants to see Benjy, all you have to do is take away my boys colors. I'm going to be there. Well, Victor, Charlie, and Joey come back to the Bronx. My brother Victor says, "Yo, Benjy! The Hell's Angels took our colors! Right, Charlie?!" "Yeah!" "Right, Joey?!" "Yeah!" "Who?! The Hell's Angels are in New York?" I said. And you know, I was already ecstatic about the Hell's Angels. I was like, "Oh, man, where are they?" "They're down on East 3rd Street," Victor said.

Two or three days later, two guys from the Hell's Angels motorcycle club come to the Bronx. It was Prince of Darkness and New Jersey. Two of them. They come right up in front of Ghetto Brothers territory. How they'd find it, I don't know. "We wanna see your leader," one of them says to the guys out front. So one of the Ghetto Brothers said, "What do you want him for?" "We have a message for him." "Yo, Benjy!" I hear from up front. I said, "What is it?" The two Hell's Angels come in. All of the guys were looking at them. And they were surrounded by all of these guys in the Bronx. Two white boys — taking a big chance coming on our turf. But they didn't look the LEAST BIT scared. So we're looking like this, like we're not worried about a thing either, and I say, real cool like,

"Can I help you?" One of them says, "Sandy wants to see you." Sandy, from the Hell's Angels, the leader of the Hell's Angels in New York. "Why?" I said. They didn't say why. So I said, "O.K., I'll take the invitation."

Now Manny Dominguez, who was a teacher at one time at Junior High School 133, and his wife, Rita, who did the film with Henry Chalfant, *Flyin' Cut Sleeves*, she was a teacher, too. They said, "We'll take you there, Benjy." So, it was Rita, Dominguez, myself, and Valentine, my bodyguard. One guy. One guy, my bodyguard. Come on, Hell's Angels?! I should've had more guys with me. So we all jump into Dominguez's car and go down to East 3rd Street, where the Hell's Angels were.

Soon as we get to that place, oh, my goodness. We got out of that car and I'm looking at a whole bunch of Triple H-looking guys; they all looked like Triple H, the WWE wrestler. And I'm like, oh, my goodness. And then Franky's like this, my boy, Valentine, he stood right by me! Man, he wasn't even phased. That guy was brave.

So, I'm looking like this, and someone said, "Benjy?" I said, "Yeah." It was Sandy. He says to me, "How old are you?" I said, "I'm 18." He goes, "You know you're old enough to die?!" I said, "What-are-you talking about?" He says, "The colors, Benjy. They look too much like Hell's Angels. If you put your boys at a distance and my boys over here. White rockers, red letters. White rockers, red letters. You have a skull and fire. We have a skull with wings. Come on! That's so identical."

Ironically, we were going to go on "The David Susskind Show" later that night. "The David Susskind Show" was doing a special with all the Presidents of the gangs in the

Bronx at that time. The Turbans, The Savage Skulls, Savage Nomads, all of them. So, I told him about that. He said, "I'll tell you what I'll do. I'll allow you to wear the colors, but you gotta get rid of the patch. If you go on TV and I see those colors on like they are, we're gonna go after you!" And I said, "Oh, yeah…" (Look at the way I was talking, sounding real tough. I was an outlaw at this time, right.) I said, "Oh, yeah, like that? Like you can just roll into the South Bronx?" He said, "You have no idea who you're messing with, right?" I said, "What, Hell's Angels?!" That was my attitude. I didn't care. And he was right: I didn't have any real idea who I was messing with.

So, Dominguez intervenes and says, "I'd like to say something." "You SHUT UP, and mind your business; nobody's talking to you," another Hell's Angels yells at him. I told Dominguez, "Be quiet." Because they were just about to POUNCE on him. They said, "SHUT UP, nobody's talking to YOU. We're talking to this guy." I said, "O.K., O.K., we'll see about that." Sandy said, "I'm warning you. We're gonna look at television tonight. David Susskind, channel 5. Gonna be watching. We're gonna be watching, Benjamin."

So, when I went back to the Bronx, I did a little research in the library on the Hell's Angels. Found out they had chapters from New York to California; chapters all over. They got 'em in New Zealand, Australia, England. They're one of the most vicious and well-organized motorcycle gangs in the country. And they are allies to some of the most vicious motorcycle gangs in the country. They're allies to all these gangs. And I was like, *Oh, my goodness!* Later on that night, somebody said, "Benjy, what's happening?"

I said, "Take off that patch!" If you would have seen me on that "David Susskind show," I didn't just take it off; it was ripped off! Man, I had a hole in my Lee jacket! I went just like that to the David Susskind Show, with a hole in my jacket. So the gang goes, "Benjy, man. You're gonna give into these guys?" I said, "Yo, brothers, you don't know who the hell you're messing with. These are the HELL'S ANGELS!"

I didn't really understand the full extent of who the Hell's Angels were. When I saw them in the movies and in magazines, I didn't realize that they were that big and for real. And they had influence. These guys knew PEOPLE! Sandy said to me, "Benjamin, you have know idea what we can do to a place like the South Bronx. You have NO idea." But it was cool. You know, he let me go. I went back to the Bronx. And I told the guys we were gonna change the colors.

That's the genesis of the garbage cans, the infamous Ghetto Brothers patch. That's when we said, What's our new patch? I looked at the garbage cans. "Ghetto Brothers!" The buildings where coming down full swing. The South Bronx was coming down, burning. The whole place was dirty, real trash. So I said, "Garbage cans!" Originally, I wanted to do garbage cans and buildings in the background. But that would be too much art. So I left it just plain garbage cans. That's the genesis of the Ghetto Brothers gang patch.

One thing that I did with the colors, that I shouldn't have done, was that on top of it, above the letters, I put "President." That was a BAD THING. You never do things like that. You NEVER put "President" on the back of your jacket. 'Cause if you do, then you'll be the target! If you're gonna kill somebody, that's the guy you wanna get, the President! So, everybody who wore my jacket, like my friends and my brother Victor, was a target.

When I started the GBs, it was around this time that I first started getting into trouble. And my father said, "You're gonna go to PR for three months, because I want you to stay out of trouble." So when I went out to PR, while I was gone, whoever wore my jacket in the Bronx, that's the guy who got hurt. My friend Joe, Black Joe, is in a wheelchair 'Cause some guys from another gang shot him from across the street, on 163rd Street and Prospect, from the rooftop. BANG!!!! These guys from another club shot him right in the spine. And to this day, Black Joe's in a wheelchair. This happened because at that time, the gang rivalries were starting to pick up, and the gangs were starting to come up strong and wild. By 1970, the Ghetto Brothers grew to at least 50 guys around the immediate area.

Between 1967 and 1973, everybody was in a gang. Remember, we were close friends. So a lot of us went to the same school. In EVERY interval in those communities there was a gang. In every interval! In those days, when I looked left, remember what God told Abraham, "Look as far as you can. Whatever's there it's yours." If I looked left, there were gangs there. If I looked right, there were gangs there. If I looked forward, there was gangs here. If I looked backward, there were gangs there. If I looked up, there was gangs there. There were gangs all over the place! Everybody had their turf. EVERYBODY was in a gang. The biggest gang in those days was the Black Spades.

VERY big. Over time, our new numbers grew, too. And it wasn't a matter of if you joined a gang, it was when.

Joining a gang was a means of survival. It was also about having power. And it was also about family. A lot of parents didn't care for their children. Parents weren't around, and a lot of times there were single parents. And if there were parents, they just didn't or couldn't care for the kids. The kids felt neglected, didn't have anybody, you know. So gangs took people like that in. But the Ghetto Brothers, when I took them in, I was thinking about their lives, as opposed to manipulating them. We didn't do that. I didn't do that. I took it to the point where I really cared for my brothers. A lot of other gangs, they used their guys to do their bidding. I never did that. But in the beginning, I have to admit, we recruited guys just like all the other gangs.

When people moved to the block, you know, you have a building, that if somebody just moved in. Like for instance, let's say a guy named Joe moved into the building in the neighborhood on the block. I'd say, "Hi, your name is Joe? O.K., my name is Benjy. You know this is Ghetto Brothers territory?" "Uh-huh, *and*?" "Well, we want you to be in it." "But what if I—" "No, you don't want to say that." So when we start with the little terrorist acts, oh, man. And then you know how we do it? It's like this, "If you don't join our gang, we're going to your apartment and we're going to break down the door and do what we have to do." Then they're like, "Nah, man, O.K., I'll join." That's how we did it. That was the gang days.

The other guys, how they did it, it was similar. All the gangs had that similar thing. Because it's all about power.

How many members you can garter. So in our community, remember, we were on big avenues.

Most gangs had age requirements, too. For the Ghetto Brothers, it was 13 and up. You had to be at least 13 to be in the Ghetto Brothers. That's why my brother Robert was never in the Ghetto Brothers. He used to hang around with me, but he was too young to join in the beginning. My brother was like a biographer, though. The guy has an incredible memory. But he was younger. I didn't allow junior Ghetto Brothers. A lot of gangs had junior members, though. Again, it was about having numbers because you had to keep up with the other clubs; so many rivalries.

We had several different rivalries at that time. We had the Dirty Dozens. The Dirty Dozens were 12 guys originally. And I remember, those guys were, on I think, Longfellow and Longwood. They had cars. I mean, these guys were bad dudes, you know what I mean. But they didn't look for trouble, but if trouble came to them, they were gonna meet you half way.

The Dirty Dozens were made up of members who were both Spanish and black. On their patch, they had the Puerto Rican and Black flag. On the car, they had the Puerto Rican and the Black flag. But remember, most of the gangs in the Bronx were composed of blacks and Spanish — Puerto Ricans mostly, some Cubans. That's how pretty much most gangs were in the Bronx, racially and ethnically mixed. The Black Spades were mostly black, some Puerto Ricans, but mostly black. The only gangs that were all one race or ethnicity were the white ones. But all of us, we were smart. You want allies. Plus, we lived among each other and were friends. We were all in the same boat, you know. We understood the city was against us; we knew we had to stick together. And that's one main thing about gangs during that time: They were all racially mixed. We knew where we stood socially and culturally.

•••

After I started the Ghetto Brothers, it wasn't too long before something happened that would force me to end the Ghetto Brothers for some time. One night, we were playing pool with a club called Magnificent Seven. We're on 158th Street. These guys owned cars; these were older men. We were playing pool, right. This guy, this older man, dressed up, wearing a suit. I beat him in a game of pool. He didn't like that.

Now, we're outside and he takes out a bowing knife — on my block! In my turf! Remember, I was into martial arts, and I had had plenty of fights by now. I didn't want to hurt him, so I said, "Listen, Sir, I don't want no problems." The guy comes at me with the knife, and my brother Robert took a pool stick. Robert's got a natural power, he's real strong. So the guy in the suit is here, and I'm here. He moves towards me with the knife. My brother Robert runs around the car, BUSHHH!!!! Cracks the guy with the pool stick. The guy falls backwards on the street, hits his head on the ground. BOOM! And I saw the blood, coming out of his head. The guy was dead instantly. I knew that right away.

I said, "Robert, he's dead!" And Ulpiano was there. I said, "Aw, man…" I had tears in my eyes. Robert said, "Benjy, I didn't mean to…" "I know you didn't mean to."

Robert was looking out for me. My brother was looking out for me. He thought the guy was gonna kill me. So we all ran home. But there were people around when it happened who saw everything.

The people in the community started to speak and someone told my father, "Don Juan, your son…" Damn. Three o'clock in the morning, my father comes into the room. We're sleeping, but not really asleep, you know, we're looking at him. He wakes my brother up. "Dress up!" "Where we going, Pa?" my brother said. "I'm taking you to the precinct. I didn't raise no criminal." That was my father for you. "I love my sons. I raised you up with the ways of God. If you're guilty, you're going to jail. If you're not, then it's up to him." "Pa, I can explain," I said. "You, SHUT UP! You're responsible!" "But Pa, you don't know what happened." My father didn't say nothing.

We all dressed up. Go to the precinct. My father walks in. Here's where we learned to love and respect our pops even more. These days, parents are like, "Oh, my son would never do that." Not my father. My father said, "I never taught him this," I'm translating for the cops and my father, "I never taught this to my son. But I'm telling you, kids these days have potential to do some stupid things. If he's guilty, you take care of business. Let the law take its tow. If he's not, then let my son go."

I'm looking at this old man, I'm looking at my father in awe. What did that teach me and my brothers? He really loved us. He really cared for us. My father was not the type of guy who would say, "*Oh, not my son.*" "Outside of my house, I don't know what he does," is what my father said. "All I know is when I'm here. I teach them to love their neighbors, to do good. To kill? Never. Murder? Worse!"

So my brother had to stay one night in jail. I explained everything. The case went for a whole year, then they dropped the case. They let my brother go. The case goes through the court a whole year, but they dropped the case because they found out that #1, Robert did it in self-defense, protecting his brother. And #2, the other thing we found out later on, is that somebody on that block, which was in Ghetto Brothers territory, 2nd Division, somebody said that the man had said, "I'm gonna dress up, 'cause tonight is gonna be the day I'm gonna die." You know Puerto Ricans, they believe in strange things. So somebody told us that he said that. The guy was LOOKING to die that night, and he put on a suit and got dressed up for the occasion.

Two or three days later after that man in the suit died, guys from Magnificent Seven came back to our turf in cars. Who are they looking for? Ghetto Brothers! Guess who they find? Not the Ghetto Brothers — The Savage Nomads! I started the Savage Nomads two or three days later, after my brother killed that guy. I said, "Guys, let's drop the Ghetto Brother colors." 1970 was the beginning of Savage Nomads.

At the time that we changed to the Savage Nomads, it was only three, four, five divisions of Ghetto Brothers. And those divisions, I sent R.C., who later became a Savage Skull, Ulpiano, Willie Vasquez. I told them, "Get me the Presidents, Vice Presidents, and Warlords of all the other divisions. We're gonna have a meeting." It was right after my birthday, August 3rd. They all came to the basement, "What's up, Benjy?" "Take off the colors. We're not going to be Ghetto Brothers anymore." "I don't want Ghetto Brothers." Then I explained the whole story of what happened with my brother and the Magnificent Seven.

O.K., so they started to change their colors. I did Savage Nomads with the skull and the fire. We were on Stebbins Avenue and 165th Street in the basement. That was the time that Charlie introduced me to Black Benjie, not Black Benjie who died, I'm talking about Black Benjie from the Savage Nomads. So Black Benjie stayed in my club for a while. He was from St. Thomas. Hangin' out. You see him in the film *Flyin' Cut Sleeves*. He's the one that coined that phrase, "Flyin' Cut Sleeves". So, one day I come with the colors. And I say, "Benjie." He looked up, he was on the sofa, "Yeah, Benjy?" "You're a Nomad!" "No, I don't wanna get involved with that." I threw the jacket at him. *"You're a Savage Nomad!"* From then on, he became a Nomad.

Then what happened? Some Ghetto Brothers started to rebel! They said, "But, yo, Benjy, man—" "Take 'em off! If you don't like it, then start your own stuff." The guys submitted. Everybody started to wear the Nomads colors. I couldn't do it by myself. They had to get their own artist. There was a skull… "That's what it looks like, guys. Ulpiano's gonna do one division. You guys get your own artist. It's a skull with fire, white and red letters." So, from then on, we became Nomads.

Then I said, "Guys, this is the new policy. Same thing with the Ghetto Brothers. Somebody jumps you, we all get on his case. There's no such thing as a clean fight anymore. When you hit, you hit to hurt!" If new guys move into a building on our turf, we knock on the door, "You just moved in?" "Yeah, yeah." "Listen, we're Savage Nomads. You're gonna be one of us!" "I'm not getting involved with that." "You better get involved! Or you're not gonna have no apartment." You could see it, the fear on their face. So they became Nomads. That's how we did it. We recruited by being terrorists! They saw all these guys, and the fact that we were downstairs, they knew that, "Aw, man, if I don't join this, then I'm going to be a victim over here."

So, from Ghetto Brothers, after what happened with my brother, we went to Nomads. Now, things were even WORSE! Now, I had to live Savage Nomad! Same initiation. But now, we had to be even a step meaner. You know why, 'cause I told the guys, "You gotta be savages, guys." "Why's that?" "Look at the name. 'SAVAGE!' We gotta act this way." So we were becoming outlaws.

When we became Nomads, the first thing we did, walking down the street, people looking, "Oh, look, they changed… What is this Savage Nomads? Where's the Ghetto Brothers?" And we went like this, "There is no Ghetto Brothers around here. We chased them outta here!"

So here I am, being a savage, right. Just being mean for no reason. There was this one time I had a hockey stick, and we were sitting down, me, Black Benjie, and some of the other guys. And I'm looking at this bus full of young people. And I'm looking at the last window, and there's a guy sitting there, mouthing off to me, making faces, you know, mouthing off something to me. And the other guys are like, "Yo, you gonna let this guy get away with that?" *Nah, I'm not gonna let him get away with that.*

I get up, walk towards the bus, it was on 163rd Street and Westchester, the bus was right there. And we were sitting on these steps. So I took the steps, got on the bus, and walk through the crowded bus to the back where this guy was sitting. I said, "You looking at me?" And I slammed the hockey stick I was carrying above and to the side of him. I broke the window where he was sitting. People started screaming and running off the bus. Everybody ran, even the bus driver tried to run. I told the bus driver, "Don't move!" And I told the guys, "Don't let him off." I was a Savage Nomad at the time. More of my guys came on the bus through the back. I said to the guy who was mouthing off, "You wanna mouth off, now?" "No, no..." And I crashed the other window right by him. "Oh, boy, you lucky," I said. I didn't hit him, but I broke the whole glass. I was just about to do this guy in. But something in me said, *Don't do it!* You know, because there were witnesses, and they were looking dead at me. But the witnesses probably wouldn't have said anything anway. Something just told me not to hit this guy. So we walked off and the guys said, "Aw, Benjy, you should've hit him, man." "Nah, man, I already did enough damage." Cops came along, we didn't run. We WALKED up the block. The cops didn't do anything.

If the cops were intimidated by us, imagine how the people felt. The people on our block loved us and feared us at the same time. They loved us because we were cool guys. But they feared us because they knew if they crossed any of us, something stupid was gonna happen.

After a while, I didn't like having to be Savage Nomads, that I had to live that life — the gang. I didn't wanna live Savage Nomad. But we just went to a level that got even worse. Now, we were going to certain areas looking for trouble. We would sit somewhere and just wait. If a guy came by, "Yo, what'you looked at him like that for, man?" Not taking peoples money, we never did that. But we would walk up to them and surround them and intimidate them. Do a number on them. But the ones we used to really start trouble with were the cops. We would go up on the roofs, with big bricks, you know the bricks that are around trees? And we would throw them at the cops. The cop cars in those days were dark green and white on the top, with the cherry ball siren on the top. So the object was to hit the cherry. "Oh, they're right there!" BOOM!!!! And we'd all run. Remember, the roofs were all stuck together. So they'd come up here, and by the time they got up to the roof where we were, we'd all be downstairs. So they knew us for smashing cop cars. So now when cops started to come in the area, they would go in circles, as opposed to stopping on a main avenue. But now, I said to the guys, "We gotta stop this." Because we were doing a routine. They're gonna know we're doing it. Later, they started having cops on the roofs. We didn't do it all the time, 'cause I knew they were gonna catch us sooner or later.

One day, I'm looking up and I said, "Yo, man, the cops are up there!" They would knock on peoples apartments. They asked me once, "Listen, is anybody…" And I lived in one of the apartments. "Uh, no, no…" "I hear people go to these roofs." "Nobody goes to the roofs!" "Are you lying to me, sir?" "I live here, come on." They didn't know it was me. So, it's things like that that people knew us for. We used to intimidate policemen and anybody else.

But we weren't the only gang that intimidated the cops. I remember one day, we saw the Black Spades, and we were sitting and checking them out. The cops stopped one of them, they surrounded the cop: "Yo, officer, you arrest him, we're gonna jump you!" I turned to the guys, I said, "Yo, did you hear this?!" The Spades were looking at us, we were looking at them. No trouble. Just looking at each other. They knew they were on neutral ground. Savage Nomads was right here. Westchester's here. Black Spades were all the way down Castle Hill, you know what I mean. So the thing is, all of the gangs, the main gangs, intimidated the cops.

But to be honest, we intimated everybody. That's what it was like. You had to live that savage life, that gang life. And just like any other gang in the Bronx, to us, turf was important Oh, man, if you pass around our turf, we didn't go around other turfs to start war, but we were looking forward to any gang to pass by our turf. You came to our turf, the first thing I'd do, I'd question you; I wouldn't jump you. I'd say, "What are you doing in my turf, man?" "What do you mean?" "This is Savage Nomads territory. You got your colors flyin', my brother. If it was over here, O.K. But you're defying, like you wanna do something."

This one time, we surrounded a guy. At first, he was like, "Nah, man, nah." But then, you know what really got me going? It's what he said that got me so angry. He said, "Yeah, I'm in your turf. So what! What you gonna do?" When you say things like that, *'What you gonna do?'* I'm gonna have to back up my words and show you what we're about. So we do this guy in. We stomped him out! Right there, in the middle of the street.

These were the sort of everyday things that we did, you know. Like there was this one time, I'm walking out of the movie theater with Beast and Louie. Now, Beast and Louie were the President and Vice President of the 2nd division of the Ghetto Brothers — The Ghetto Brothers gang after we changed back from the Nomads. The 2nd division was on Trinity Avenue. So, we're walking out to the street — we had been watching a Hell's Angels movie, *Hell's Angels on Wheels*. So I was already inspired, you know, the movie had hyped me up even more. Remember, I'm savage at this point. So we're walking out, and we see some mopeds, about four or five of them, in the front. And then I'm the one who said, "Yo, Beast, check out those mopeds, my brother." He said, "Yeah, they look cool." "Take it!"

There was a guy sitting on one of the mopeds. His boys were still in the movies. They didn't come out, it was just him. And I said, "Yo, I like your bike." And the guy said, "Yeah, so what about it? What are you gonna do?" See, when you say things like that, that's when it happens!

So Beast grabbed the guy and they started to fight. Then that guy threw my boy. Now they were really going at it. So one of this guy's boys comes out and jumps on top of Beast. So Louie and I took that guy and pulled him around and Beast jumped at him. Ooo, when I say, "Beast!" Man, my boy, Beast — his real name was Angel — was a BEAST! He was a big dude, man. Anyway, the rest of this guy's boys never came out the movie. Me and Louie were looking, and Louie said, "If they come out, we got this, here." Nothing happened. We never took his bike. But we did those guys in big time.

This is how it was. I remember there was a fight on Prospect Avenue. My brother — the one who killed a guy — threw a guy through a window. I forget the name of the restaurant, the Crab Store, the Crab Restaurant, something like that. So, he got into an altercation with some guys. They were not a gang, they were just a group of dudes who wanted to hang out. So, we got into a fight. The ones who usually started the fight was my two brothers. They were the troublemakers! Whatever they did, I had to finish it. So, my brother stood there, and the guy punches my brother. My brother said, "Aw, you can do better than that." He hit my brother hard, I mean square in the jaw. So Robert picked him up, threw the guy right through the window! And there was a guy in the restaurant who knew my father. "Wait 'til I tell your father!" So my father had to pay for that window. Right through the glass, Robert throws this guy. I come up from City Island and my father says to me, "Benjy, your brother Robert threw a guy through the glass." "A gang?" I said, 'cause I'm thinking war. "No, no, some guys just hanging out. He punched your brother, and your brother just threw him through the glass." Now see, that involves the other guys to take action. Which they did. When I wasn't there, and the other guys took over the Nomads, they just did a number on these guys with pool sticks. And then who gets the brunt of it? Me.

When that situation happened, around that same time, I'm looking out on the street and I see some of my guys, "Yo, Benjy. We caught this guy on our turf." I'm looking at him. It was Blackie! That's how I was introduced to Blackie for the first time. That's Blackie who was the long-time leader and President of the Savage Skulls. My boys bring him to me. And see, Blackie thinks there's something wrong with this story. He says when we caught him, we were Ghetto Brothers. But we were not Ghetto Brothers. We were Nomads at that point; I hadn't restarted the Ghetto Brothers yet. And I asked my brother Robert about it. He confirmed it. I said, "Robert, when we caught Blackie, what were we?" He said, "We were Savage Nomads." I knew it. I was right. I asked another guy who used to paint my jacket, Piano. "Piano, you were the ones who brought Blackie?" "Yeah." "What were we Piano in those days?" "Oh, we were Savage Nomads."

Blackie was on Rogers Place when my boys caught him. He had a lee jacket with a demon in the middle, a devil. 'Cause that was a famous patch. Everybody used to wear those. So Blackie and I became friends; we were just talking. I don't know what gang Blackie was in at that time. I think it was the Demons or something. So I already had a drawing and the colors for a gang called the Savage Skulls. I said, "Blackie, look at that drawing." What did he see? Savage Skulls. I had two drawings. On the paper, I had Savage Nomads. And then, on this side of the drawing, same drawing, I have it in my house somewhere, I had Savage Skulls. He looked at it. He said, "Benjy, can I have that?" I never forgot that. I said, "Sure, go ahead." So he took it. Blackie used the name and colors I created, which he slightly changed, and he started the Savage Skulls. I don't want for there to be any confusion about this. I wasn't the founder of the Savage Skulls. I just came up with the name and original colors. Blackie gets all the credit for founding the Savage Skulls and building that gang into what they became.

When I left the Nomads, my brother Victor stood with the Savage Nomads. He came back when I started the Ghetto Brothers again in 1971. We became Ghetto Brothers again and Victor left the Nomads and came back to the Ghetto Brothers. Then Black Benjie took over the Nomads.

The full history is this: I had the Savage Skulls in '66, but it was only these 15 guys. I dropped that, then I started the Ghetto Brothers in '67, with the colors. It was '66, yeah, Savage Skulls was first drawn up in '66. After Blackie asked for my Savage Skulls drawing in the basement, he took it from that point on, as I was with the Savage Nomads. Then it was later on, 1971, when I started the Ghetto Brothers again.

• • •

In 1971, when I was just starting to catch glimpses of politics, I left the Savage Nomads and started the Ghetto Brothers again. My brother Victor stayed and took over the Savage Nomads when I left. After that one year as Savage Nomads, my father sent me away for three months. He feared for me because I was getting into trouble. He still didn't know that I was in a gang. He just knew that I kept getting into trouble. I went to Puerto Rico. When I came back to the Bronx, I found out that my brother Victor was stabbed in the back several times and once close to his chest. He was wearing my colors that said "President." We were still Savage Nomads then. He had taken over the Nomads when I left. Black Benjie told me, "Yo, Benjy, when you left and your brother took over, this guy was a tyrant!" Victor was like, *My brother's not here,*

I'm going to call the shots here. And that's how he ran the gang, like a tyrant.

So when I got back from Puerto Rico, I'm looking at my brother Victor; he's already healed. I said, "Yo, Victor, you O.K., man?" "Yo, Benjy, I'm good, man." "Who did this to you, Victor?" "The Saints!" "The Saints did this to you?!" This guy, Saint, was the main dude in this gang called the Saints. Yo, these guys were no joke. Saint was a Skinny guy. He could run. He was a black brother. Like a military leader. This guy was NO JOKE! The Saints had St. Mary's park. If you go there, don't mess with these guys, 'cause you ain't never gonna come out. I got my friend, Kong — King Kong — look at the names, Louie, Beast, Piano, Tahto. "Let's go in the car." "Where we going, Benjy?" "We're going to St. Anne's." See, I came back from Puerto Rico as the same guy. I still had that savage in me. Soon as we get to St. Anne's and we open the doors, we were on their turf, they were like, "Oh, shit! Savage Nomads!" They thought we were coming with an invasion; but it was only five of us.

So I'm looking for the guys who stabbed my brother. Saint! I never forgot that name. I'm looking at these guys. They were the same guys who beat up my friend Herc. Skinny guy, very powerful kid. They jumped him one day when he was alone in the park. So they were doing the same thing we used to do. Not one on one. They jumped everybody at the same time. Herc comes up the block and he falls on me, "Yo, Benjy, the Saints jumped me." We went back again, couldn't find them. I said, "Damn, we gotta get these guys."

After I started the Ghetto Brothers again, we started to grow much bigger than before. I tried to get my brother to rejoin the Ghetto Brothers. "Hey, Victor, come over here." So he left, became a Ghetto Brother again, and Black Benjie took over the Savage Nomads. At this time, we had our clubhouse. The Ghetto Brothers clubhouse was on a ground floor. You know, it was like a grocery store. The city paid for it. YSA — Youth Services Agency. But they didn't know what we were really doing incognito. The city wanted to get the gang leaders out of the streets. They gave us a club. They paid for the rent, they paid for the phone, and they paid us, the leaders. They paid for everything just to keep us out of trouble. But at night time, we changed. The city only did this for the bigger gangs, the ones that were known, well recognized. All the leaders were paid, not the members. As long as you pay off the leader, you got it made because that's the people you go to. The leader's supposed to put everything in control.

You ever heard of Equitable Insurance Company? They donated a T.V. to us. They gave us a color television. I said, "Yo, guys, look! We got a T.V." Everybody went crazy, cheering and stuff, you know. Every gang didn't have a clubhouse. Only the main gangs, some of the main leaders. Like you got for example, the Bachelors, Savage Skulls, Savage Nomads, the principle gangs, not the little guys, the MAIN guys. And we even had a Youth Service Rep. He would come down to check out what we were doing. He would take notes and everything. The guy was an Irishmen. We used to call him "Red." But Red was well-informed about all the gangs. I remember one time, I went to his office downtown and I was talking to him and I said, "So, Red, what's up with the Chinese gangs?" He said, "You don't wanna mess with those guys. Those guys are not playing. You go into their community, you're never going to come out."

And the thing about the clubhouse that the city paid for, they didn't know what we were doing incognito. The city didn't know to what extent how bad we were, how all the gangs were. They thought by giving us clubhouses and paying for stuff, we'd quiet down. But remember, we were a *gang*, which meant we did stuff like every other gang in the South Bronx. We had our rumbles like everybody else, you know. And every gang had its own Warlord.

The purpose of the Warlord, first, if the Presidents of the two gangs can not see eye to eye, then the Vice Presidents have to jump in and see if they can come up with a better solution. If they didn't come up with a better solution, and they were adamant about fighting, you know, rumbling, then the guy who's the Warlord — who knew skilled fighting, he was a skilled fighter, good in strategy — he would set up everything. Now, he called the shots. The Warlord got everybody ready, trained the guys. The Warlord was usually one of the best fighters in the gang, if not *the* best fighter in the gang.

The Warlord would agree to the time and place for the rumble. If you're not there, you forfeit your colors. So you have to give 'em up. That means, victory! But if it's gonna happen, we gotta be in the place where it's not too many people. Like back in an alley somewhere. 'Cause the people are gonna call the cops, and they're gonna arrest us.

The first Warlord of the Ghetto Brothers was Franky Valentine. Franky Valentine, very talented guy. Great drawer, he used to draw. Great congas player. Puerto Rican guy. He was a short guy. If you see the Ghetto Brothers album cover, *Power Fuerta*, if you look at the guy with the hat on, next to my brother on your right, that's Franky. So Franky became the first Warlord of the Ghetto Brothers. A very nice guy, but when he did plans, he did it cool. He'd plan very well.

And most of the time, Franky said, "Weapons is not necessary." You know why? Because I told him, "We don't need weapons. That's gonna put brothers away. Lets' use our hands." So, how is this gonna happen? We don't need the weapons, 'cause somebody's gonna get killed. Let's just go with the hands. But in most cases, when it did happen, when we did go with the hands; somebody from the other side, and maybe some of my boys here, might turn up with a blade, or a broken bottle, or a bat, or some other weapons. So when you're in the heat of battle, you can't stop now. You've got to take your chances. You deal with that when you get back to the club.

There were a couple of rumbles where I said, "What happened? You could've killed this dude, man! It's gonna get worse." We usually didn't want it to escalate, but it happened sometimes. That was the era: violent chaos! So, Franky and I and the guys got together and said, Why don't we try to do it with leader against leader. But maybe the other leader doesn't want to fight. The other leader says, "Nah, nah, I don't want that." Because maybe he sees that this leader looks like he's a better fighter. So, instead of designating one of his boys, he says, "We're gonna do this together, a rumble, right?" Cause this guy's like, "I'm not going down alone." So, none of that. The other leaders have to save face. So no man against man, leader against leader. It's gotta be a rumble. And if the weapons come out, it's like I said, in the heat of the battle, you can't stop. You gotta rumble! Of course, some brothers got hurt; some brothers got badly hurt; some got killed. But a lot of them survived.

The Ghetto Brothers were known for being good with the hands; that's one of things we were known for. So the fear for a lot of the other gangs was this: Since the Ghetto Brothers were good with the hands, good wrestlers, boxers, martial arts, a lot of these guys from other gangs always wanted to use weapons when they rumbled with us.

People knew what we were capable of because when we approached them, *we approached them*! We used to hang out in the parks, and we used to talk to each other. There were times that you could come to a neutral turf. The neutral turf was really the Ghetto Brother's area. Ghetto Brothers, from the outset I said, "Any gang could come here. Just don't start any trouble." And then they would ask questions, "What kind of guns you guys got? You know, 'cause we got sawed-off shot guns, .38s. .45s." I'd say, "We don't carry those things, man." See, and the word spread out. But it wasn't hard to get guns in the South Bronx if you needed them.

Savage Skulls knew us for that. Savage Nomads, Black Benjie knew us for that. The Bachelors knew us for that. The Black Spades, The Roman Kings. They all said, the Ghetto Brothers are known mainly for the hands. And so, the guys would tell them, "Nah, man, we don't use them 'cause the President don't want us to use weapons. Our weapons is our hands." That's why a lot of these guys didn't want to confront us face to face. Their thing was, if I could shoot you, we'd be better off.

So, me and my boys, we were always training EVERYDAY. And you know how we used to do it? We use to go to the Jackson Housing Projects. We announced that we were going to have exercises. War exercises. So the 2nd Division was ready for the 1st Division, which is us, going to the projects. And here's how it was. It wasn't a little tit for tat. If you see me, you jump me. And I mean, you GIVE IT to me! It was so bad one time that the people from the projects, Jackson Projects, called the cops. Hey, there's a gang fight here! It was just us doing exercises, but nobody was holding back. And then when the cops came. Some guys had broken noses. Some brothers had there fingers broken. Some guys got their ribs broken. Because I said, "If we're gonna rumble, let's do this for real." That was our exercises.

I thought with a military mind, with planning and strategy. One time I said to the guys, "If I wanted to really get somebody, the best time to get them is in the winter or the 4th of July." Ghetto Brothers looked at me, "Benjy?! Winter?" "Winter, yeah. Nobody hangs out." Where are the guys in the winter time? They're in the club. You want to assassinate them? That's the best place to do it. Second, the 4th of July. "Benjy, why the 4th of July?" "Easy. Firecracker, .22 caliber hand gun. Same sound. M-80 fireworks, shot gun. Same sound." So everybody thinks it's a celebration when you hear all of that, but what you're really doing is shooting. During that time, I was always thinking up war strategies. But I never pursued most of that. But that's where my mind was at, and that's where I could have gone with it because that's who I was at that time.

But we didn't war with everybody. We had our allies, like the Turbans. We were all close together. These guys were BAD GUYS! Nice guys — Don't cross them! If you look at their women wrong, forget it. These guys were known to PUT YOU AWAY! You know. If you come to their turf, you ain't getting out! Once you say, "We're gonna fight with The Turbans, they ain't gonna let you go. They caught a guy in the hallway. I forgot which gang he was from. I think he was a Royal Javelin. They caught him in the hallway. They told me, "Yo, Benjy, they killed the guy in there." The guy came into Turban territory. That's why I told my guys, "Don't go into Turban territory. You're never gonna come out! When they get you, that's it." The Turbans didn't believe in taking prisoners or talking it out. Once they get you, you're out! But out of all those guys, Chino's the only survivor.

The Turbans were veterans, Vietnam veterans. These guys did not have little guns, these guys had RIFLES! We were gonna rumble with the Royal Javelins, they came to our aid. And I'm looking like this, I said, "Look at these guys. They're bringing out riffles!" These were older guys. You don't mess with these guys. Even though we had more members than them. But remember, I always respected my elders.

Chino was respected, and Manny, the leader, both were well respected. You know what Manny did, in front of me? It was right in their turf. They caught this guy from another gang. "Yo, man, yo, man, we got this guy. Oh, this how you deal with it…" BOOM! "You kill the guy!"

And that's not it. He got certain guys in his community together. He said he wanted to have a meeting. Took them to Turban territory, CLICK, CLICK: "All you guys are gonna be Turbans." They came to us one day with the idea of doing the same thing, making us all Turbans. You know the trailer, where they put the music in the parks? Where you play on stage? The Ghetto Brothers were playing — the Ghetto Brothers band — we were playing on stage, doing a song, and we see The Turbans coming. They were marching, like the Black Panthers, they were coming in line. So we stopped playing. I jumped off the stage; all the Ghetto Brothers were there. Manny, Chino, and I, we shook hands, both gangs on opposite sides of the other. Manny says to me, "Yo, Benjy. It would be nice if you guys become Turbans." I said, "It would be nice if you guys become Ghetto Brothers." No altercation. We hugged and shook hands. From then on, we had big mutual respect for each other. Because it was understood: We were all outlaws.

Chapter 5
Flying Colors

EVERYBODY in the South Bronx was flying colors in the late '60s, early '70s! These were some crazy times. All the gang wars. And somebody was always taken somebody's colors. This gang, these clubs over here, taking the colors from these guys over there. A lot of the time, that's how gang wars started: somebody taking somebody's colors.

One time, this gang took my boy's colors, they took my boy's colors, Piano. Every gang knew me, Benjy from the Ghetto Brothers; I didn't always know about them, but they knew me from my reputation. "You want Benjy here?" "Yeah." "Take one of his boys' colors." You take one of my boys' colors, I WOULD BE THERE TO SEE YOU MYSELF, you could count on that!

So soon as they took my boy Piano's colors, it was the Royal Javelins, I went on my bicycle with Piano, he was right behind me. We stopped at 174th Street and Boston Road, the Boys Club was up the block. Me and Piano were in Turban territory, but the Javelins were up the block, their turf was up the block. As soon as we got to the corner, I looked around, I saw some guys coming toward me. "Who are you?" They said to us. "Ghetto Brothers," I said. "Off the bike!" the guy said, as he pulled a gun on me. I said, "Yo, man…" He pulled a gun on me, right there in the STREET! BROAD DAY LIGHT! I said, "Yo, man, we don't take off our colors for nobody. Right, Piano?" Soon as I turn around, Piano already had his colors off. I was like, "Aw, man. All right, here you go…" So they said, "Let's go!" I said, "Where we going?" "We're going to the club." I said to myself, *aw, man*. I looked at Piano. In my mind — I didn't tell him — but I said to myself, *They're gonna kill us*. I just knew they were gonna kill us. Because that was how it was then.

We were on the Turbans turf, so we would have been all right. But there were no Turbans that were there at the time. If the Turbans would've seen us, they would've come to help us. But they were not there. The Royal Javelins caught us before any Turbans showed up. So they took us from 174th Street and Boston Road to their turf on Jennings. We're walking and while they were walking in the street, they took our bikes, they were messing them up. They were holding up our Ghetto Brothers colors like they'd just won some big victory. And then, this girl said, "Ghetto Brothers?!" The guy says, "Yeah, yeah." She says, "Did you kill them?" I was like, *Aw, man*. As soon as she said that, they said, "No, they're right here." And they looked at me. I was terrified. I knew she had just hyped them up even more!

So we went down the stairs into their clubhouse. As soon as we go downstairs, I see the President, Reuben. I'm looking at him, he says, "Benjy?" I said, "Your boys, man." "What's up?" "Your boys in your 3rd division on Claremont Avenue are starting trouble with my boys." He said, "Damn, Benjy, all you had to do was ask me. I can control my boys. I can just simply say, 'Stop!' But yo, look at your boys, too, my brother. Look at your boys, too." See, it was about leadership. Our responsibility was to stop our boys, to avoid all the problems if we could. That was each gang leader's responsibility.

So then Reuben said, "Give Benjy back his colors." 'Cause I was a cool guy, man. I was a very nice person, despite the gang stuff, you know. But I didn't come around all rowdy. I was mostly calm. So they give us back our colors, right. And I had a soda in my hand and I said, "You want some Soda?" to one of their guys, 'cause I heard one of the Royal Javelins say he was thirsty. Guy goes, "I don't drink Ghetto Brothers soda!" I was like, *Ghetto Brothers soda?* I looked at Piano, we both wanted to laugh so bad. So they give us back our bikes.

When we went back to the block, the block was full of several different gangs. The rumor was: "They caught Benjy!" So the guys on the block had mobilized for war! "Benjy, we were just about to go to Jennings Street and start a war," one of the GBs said. I said, "For what? I told you I was just going to get the colors." So everything calmed down. But that's how quickly things could escalate.

Four or five days later, the Ghetto Brothers from Claremont had a war with the Javelins. That was the 3rd division of the GBs. That's on Claremont Avenue. So they had a fight with some of the Javelins. And guess what happened? Some Ghetto Brothers… When you take a person's colors, what does it mean? Victory? When you take their colors and hang 'em on a poll, you're saying, I took their flag! Guess what The Javelins did? In Ghetto Brothers territory, cops came up to me, "All right, Benjy, give them back their colors." "WHAT?!" We all started to laugh. They called the cops on us?!!!! NO GANG IS SUPPOSED TO DO THAT! That's a cardinal rule. You don't go to the cops and tell them, "Go to the Ghetto Brothers and tell them to give back our colors." NO GANG IS SUPPOSED TO TELL THE COPS ABOUT ANOTHER GANG. Not about a rumble, a war, nothing! You don't tell the cops nothing! We were all flying colors, and that was the code, man. You don't talk to the cops about nothing.

When the other gangs found out what the Royal Javelins did, everybody was like, *Aw, man, that's not too cool.* So we said, "Here, give them to the cry babies. Take 'em, get outta here." And I found out later on that my cousins were in the Royal Javelins. My two cousins, they're coming up the block, "Yo, Benjy!" And I'm looking out the window on 163rd Street, "What is it?" GBs say to me, "We got two Javelins here." I looked and said, "Those are my cousins, man. Come upstairs." They come upstairs. MayLin was there, she said, "Benjy, stop this, man." She thought that I was going to hurt them. She didn't know that they were my cousins. I said, "Guys come in. Hey, Tonchi and Louie, you guys Royal Javelins?" "Yeah, we told 'em that you're our cousin." "Why don't you join the Ghetto Brothers?" "Nah, man, we live over there." "O.K., fine." They were my cousins. What am I gonna do? I'm not gonna hurt my cousins.

So, after that, the Royal Javelins were looked down upon for what they did — calling the cops. NO GANG DID THINGS LIKE THAT! Just like, if you did something to one of my boys and you murder him, we're not supposed to talk to the cops, like, "He did it!" We don't do that, 'cause we take care of it ourselves. When that thing jumped off, we thought about it, but at the same time we said, "Nah, you know what, it's time." So for now on, when we go to war with them, we don't take their colors 'cause they're gonna call the cops.

• • •

The 7th division of the Ghetto Brothers was my military division. These guys were very stubborn. They wanted to keep their weapons. They said, "No, Benjy we don't want to get rid of our weapons." I said, "I don't wanna see no weapons here." But that was the 7th division, which was on University Avenue. They were so big, the Ghetto Brothers 7th division, they had A, B and C sub-divisions. They were broken down into different divisions within the division.

In that division of Ghetto Brothers, there was at least 300 or 400 guys. There were a LOT of guys in those divisions. That's why I used to call them my military wing of the Ghetto Brothers. But these guys, I kept them at bay — oh, my goodness. Karate Tony, the leader of that division, and these guys. Yo, I had to keep them at bay. I said, "Tony, I don't wanna find out that you guys are using weapons for this kind of crap. Please, don't do this."

Now, something happened with the Ghetto Brothers 7th divisions. University Avenue. I go there one day. As soon I walked into the club, they pushed me in. I turned and looked, it was the cops! Detectives. And they went, "Who's this guy?" Ghetto Brothers said, "Nah, that's one of my boys." Then the cop yelled, "I WANT THE PRESIDENT OF THE GHETTO BROTHERS! WHERE THE HELL IS HE?!" Everybody tried their hardest not to look directly at me.

So, I'm off to the side, punching this board, being incognito and looking over the Ghetto Brothers, trying to figure out what's going on. As soon as the cop said that he was looking for the President of the Ghetto Brothers, all of the girls looked at me. And I shook my head at them, you know, like, *Stop looking at me!* You know, discretely. One Ghetto Brother had a beret with "GB" on it. So the cop, a black brother, said, "What does that mean?" The GB said, "It means, Good Boy." The cop said, "Oh, you wanna be funny, tough guy? Tell me you're the President of the Ghetto Brothers and I'll lock you up." He said, "I'm the President of the Ghetto Brothers." The cop goes like this, like he's going to arrest him. But he didn't. He just kept on harassing this GB.

Then the cop looked at me. He said, "Where you from?" "I'm from Prospect," I told him. "Did you just kill a Hobo the other day? I heard something." "No, sir, officer. I don't do things like that." I kept on punching the board. He said, "You look nervous." "I'm not nervous. I'm just coming to see my friends." Then, the cops left.

After the cops were gone, I turned to Tony and I said, "Tony, what the hell happened?" "Yo, Benjy, some Junior Ghetto Brothers went to this police sergeant's house and they stole his weapons." "What?" "They stole his weapons. Benjy, come here, I wanna show you something." We go to the ceiling. And the cops weapons were up there, hidden in the ceiling. I said, "No, what are you doing?!" He said, "Don't worry about it, they ain't never gonna find out." But that's what the cops were looking for. These Junior Ghetto Brothers went trick or treating. They go to this police sergeant's apartment. Soon as he opens the door,

CH-CHCK!!!! with the shot gun: "Get against the wall!" They tied the cop up and took his weapons. Tony told me the whole story. I said, "Hold it, Tony. Are you serious?"

Prior to that, some drug dealers killed a Ghetto Brother. The Ghetto Brothers of that Division said, "Well, two can play the same game." They went to an apartment where the dealers were buying dope, and was like, *Yeah, yeah:* BANG!!!! Shot the guys who killed the Ghetto Brother.

I don't remember the name of the Ghetto Brother they killed, but when news got to me, I said, "Tony, stop it, now! I don't want war on my hands, man. You're responsible for this." "All right, Ben." These guys from my 7th division were BAD dudes!

Remember, we were a gang. And I take full responsibility for creating that climate, you know. In the beginning, we were bad. I won't sugarcoat that fact. We were outlaws, we wanted to be that way. We *had* to be that way in those times. Our initiation alone, tells me, this is the warrior that I want.

Every gang had some crazy initiation. A lot of gangs had the Apache line, where you had to make it through to the end. You know, there were guys lined up on both sides with chains, sticks, and stuff, and their fists, trying to stop you from making it to the end. You had to make it through the Apache line to join most clubs. But I took it a step further because I wanted my guys to be savages. So you know what we did for initiation, besides having to get beat up to get in? Since there were a lot of abandoned buildings, you had to live in an abandoned building anywhere from two to five days, alone. You could not come out. We would bring the food to you, but you had to stay there. What's that for? To break your fear. What happens when you're sleeping in an abandoned building alone? What do you hear? Drug addicts. All kinds of people ready to rob you, kill you. You get terrified. You can be like this in a room and you hear somebody coming down and say, "Oh, who the hell is that?" So you had to stay in the abandoned building, alone, to overcome fear.

After five days, you come out. We take you to the Ghetto Brothers club. Now that your mind is right, I wanna test the warrior in you. So you had to fight at least three guys. Every gang had some initiation where you had to fight, get beat, to get in. For our initiation, you had to fight at least three guys for as long as the 45, the record, is playing. No Apache line, that's over too quick. You had to last the whole record. That means the whole song. For instance, the song "It's a Family Affair," by Sly and the Family Stone. You'd have to fight three guys while that song played. When the song finished, the fight is over. But anything goes while that song is playing.

I mean, people would get hurt, man. There was this one time, when Beast broke one of the guys' arm, the guy who was be initiated. And I said, "Oh, my goodness." And he went like, "AHHHH, AHHHH!!!!" The guy looked over to me to stop it. I said, "Nope. The record's not finished, my brother. You're going to have to keep fighting." So the guy kept swinging, kept fighting 'cause he wanted to be in the Ghetto Brothers club.

And there was another time when some GBs broke another guy's jaw. A new GB was getting initiated, getting beat up and another guy who was about to be initiated was watching. His turn was next. So, I looked. The next guy, he said, "Aw, man." He was terrified, wasn't sure if we wanted to join anymore. I said, "Yo! If you wanna change your mind, do it now." He said, "Nah, man, I'm gonna do it." "O.K., fine." I looked at my brother Victor, I said, "Victor, I'm going to the store. Put on the 45, you're in charge. I'll be right back." When I came back, he had an album on! He had an ALBUM on, Grandfunk Railroad. He's making the guy fight as long as an album's playing. And I said, "Victor, what are you doing?" He said, "I just wanted to see if the guy—" "NO! You're gonna kill this guy." And the guy was getting whipped, just torn up. He was getting beat up bad. And he's crying. He says, "Benjy, look. He put on an album, but he told me not to say nothing 'cause he said you put him in charge." I said, "Victor, get out! Get out!" I took the album, I looked at the guy, his jaw was hanging. I told some of the guys to take him to the old Lincoln Hospital. A week later, the guy comes back to the Ghetto Brothers clubhouse, bruised and bandaged up. He says, "Benjy, am I in?" "Yeah, you're in." I'm not gonna say no to the guy, he already passed the test.

So that was the warrior part. That's the climate I created. I wanted my guys to be warriors. Look at the community, look at where we were living. It was a war zone, man. You always had to be ready. There were gang members who wouldn't think twice about killing you.

So after you made it through that, after you made it through the initiation, you get your colors. Beautiful colors. Nice Lee jacket. We take it to the gasoline station. We put the jacket on the floor. And then the guys, four or five guys, would piss all over the jacket. We were supposed to be outlaws. So we'd piss all over your jacket. After that, if a guy's lucky and someone vomits on your jacket, even better. Then you take the jacket and you put it on. You have to stay with that for a week.

Now, right next to the gas station was an old oil drum. In the old days, they used to have drums full of oil. You had to dip yourself in this oil, waist high. You get out and you could not take a bath for a whole week. So you had not only colors soiled with all that crap, but you hadn't taken a bath for a week. So what did that prove? That you were an outlaw. Nobody wants to hang around you. Not even a fly.

And when you look at that, it's all these guys — dirty, filthy, mean looking. But we had to live like outlaws. Where did I get that from? Hell's Angels. I wanted to be like that. What did that do psychologically to a person? Now you see us, people are like, "Oh, my goodness, a bunch of bums. With chains." And early on, we used to carry blades right in front of the cops! Out here, you know, you're not suppose to do that.

One time, I had a blade on me. I took the knife out in the open, right in front of a cop. The cop gets out of his car, and I break it immediately. 'Cause if it's seven inches long, you get mandatory time. So I deliberately broke the knife. So the cop said, "Oh, you think you're slick?!" And the knife was in half. He said, "Benjamin, can I have that?!"

Damn, man, we used to walk around with that in the street. With the blades here, the chains here. In most cases, when people saw us this way, I wanted to test our meanness. For instance, this one time we went to Southern Boulevard and 149th Street. There was a movie house there. But there was two or three little motorcycles, you know the little motorcycles? So there was a club that was inside watching a movie.

So they came out. And we looked at them, it was The Demons. I said, "Those are your bikes?" "Yeah, what about it?!" "I like 'em." "Well, you're not gonna take 'em." "Well, maybe we don't take your bikes, but we'll take you." "Oh, you think you're like that?" "Yeah!" So, when I went this way, Beast comes in, POW!!! Smacks the guy. The guy's on the ground. Two guys there with him. I said, "Don't even make a move." 'Cause it was at least 15 of us. And we were on their turf. I said, "Don't even make a move!" So, the guy got on top of Beast. I took the guy off of Beast, then Beast went on top of him. And the Ghetto Brothers were on the side kicking the guy, just stomping him. We told the other two guys, "Don't even think about jumping in, 'cause we're gonna do the same thing to you." We did a number on the guy, and I said, "Man, you can keep your stupid bikes." After that, we walked towards St. Mary's Park, which was where they were. So word came around, *Yo, Ghetto Brothers came here and they beat him. They beat up this guy! They look like a bunch of derelicts.* But that was the psyche.

That's the life we had to live, we had to be outlaws. And remember, my father didn't know ANYTHING about me at that time. Nothing! He had no idea what I was doing. We were still observing our faith on Friday nights. Nobody knew that we were Jewish, but this was something that I was conscious of — my faith — throughout the gang era. But I never told anyone because of my father. My father thought that if he told people that we were Jewish, that if we lived outwardly as Jews, that we would get hurt. This fear passed on to me.

During the Ghetto Brothers era, when we were flying colors, the guys didn't know anything; they didn't know that I was Jewish. I never told them. Charlie — Karate Charlie — and everybody looked at me as a Pentecostal, they thought that I was a Protestant. See, my father had left the Catholic church because this other guy, who was a Protestant, introduced my father to that religion. So my father left the Catholic church and became a Protestant supposedly. "Why?" I asked. "Because they're a little better," he said. "They're a little better, as opposed to the Catholics," he said. So, we started to go to another church, again, just for show. Now, in this church, they didn't worship idols like they did in the Catholic church. No more beads, no more crosses, we don't need that. Which, in Torah, forget all of that. You know what I mean? So, it's like taking us from one religion to another. But we were never to be open about our true religion. We were not to tell anybody that we were Jewish. NEVER! This is how we had to live. This, too, was on my mind, right in the middle of living that outlaw life.

This was early, the early Ghetto Brothers, prior to the end of 1971, before I brought in peace and social activism, and changed the Ghetto Brothers to the organization. After that situation with this guy that we did the number on, we went to tell the victory to the other Ghetto Brothers. And I reminded them, "Ghetto Brothers, this is our policy. No Ghetto Brother fights alone! If you find anybody fighting with a Ghetto Brother, you all jump in and do that guy in. We'll never lose a battle that way." "But Benjy, it's not fair!" "Ah, fair nothing! Ain't NOBODY fair out here. You flying colors, ANYTHING goes, man. Once you put those colors on, anything can happen. These clubs out here won't hesitate to kill you or jump you, stab you, whatever. So what we did, that will teach every other gang member. The message is: You jump GB, you die!"

...

Even though gangs were mostly in the Bronx, there was gangs all over the city. But everywhere I went in the city, I carried that Bronx mentality with me. There was this one time when I went to Chinatown with MayLin. She was my girlfriend at the time. We went to Chinatown, I was with Táto, my boy who later on, I rescued this guy. So, we went to Chinatown and I was sitting down in the movie theater with my girlfriend, and I'm looking to my left. I see all these Chinese guys looking at me. So I was like, *Oh, boy, these are the*...I think it was the White Cranes or the White Dragons, one of those; it was a Chinese gang. The guy who was looking at me, he didn't like the fact that I was with MayLin, you know, because she was Chinese.

So after the movie was over, I'm walking up the aisle, my woman, MayLin, her cousin and my friend RC. The guy comes running behind. Three guys, the main guy and two guys behind him. He says, "Yo, what you said to me, man?" The guy had long hair. I was like, "What?! I ain't say nothin' to you, man!" I Already knew what it was about because I was with MayLin. So he said, "You wanna fight?" I said, "What?!" So I put my girlfriend to the side to keep her out of danger. As soon as I step towards him, RC goes, "I got this guy, man!" Then: BOOM!!! The

Chinese guy kicks him right in the face. He kicks RC, drops him! So I grab RC. Then the guy pulls out a gun and pulls the trigger. Nothing happens! He had it on safety. I was like, *OH, SHIT!*

So me and RC took off. MayLin and her cousin stayed, they were talking in Chinese. 'Cause I knew they weren't going to do anything to them. That's why they call me Yellow Benjy, 'cause of MayLin, because she was Chinese. There was three known Benjy's in the South Bronx at that time. I was the one who coined these two guys. Black Benjie. 'Cause there were three of us, Black Benjie from the Savage Nomads and Black Benjie from the Ghetto Brothers.

So me and RC are running till we see City Hall. Then we hopped the train and went home back to the Bronx. I got in touch with MayLin later. "They didn't do nothin' to you?" "No, Benjy, it wasn't me they wanted. It was the fact that you were with me." I wasn't Chinese. O.K., fine.

So I called a war meeting with the Ghetto Brothers. "Ghetto Brothers. Get me…I just want three Divisions." "What do you want, Benjy?" "We're gonna invade Chinatown." "Yo, Benjy, you serious?" "Yeah, yeah. But I want one particular guy. We're gonna grab this guy. We're gonna put him in a car, take him to the Bronx, and I want you guys to destroy this guy. They said, "Benjy, how do you propose to do this?" "Simple, man. Simple, we go in cars. We go and cruise around the area, man, this is their turf."

I thought about it that night and I told MayLin. MayLin looked at me and said, "Benjy, don't deal with it. These guys don't play! And they have organizations that are tight." I said, "I don't care. They offended me, they offended my honor, they offended you, and they're gonna pay for this."

Then I was talking to this guy named Red, from YSA, Youth Services Agency, under Ted Gross. They knew all about all the gangs. So I told him what I was gonna do. Red told me, "You don't wanna do that, Benjy. Let me show you something." Then he showed me statistics. "Number 1, see, Benjy. These guys have more guns than the Hell's Angels. Second, these guys are involved in the Chinese Mafia. These guys DON'T PLAY! And they're very centralized in their community. Third, if you go around that block, the Italians are next door. So you're going to have to pass these guys."

I saw the map. I looked at it, I studied it, I came back and told the Ghetto Brothers, "Cancel it!" "What happen?" "We can't do it. We're going to be massacred if we go there. These guys are the Chinese Mafia! And even if we go, we have to pass the Italians. We're gonna have to fight these guys to get to the Chinese. Nah, it ain't gonna happen." I saw in their faces that they were disappointed. The Ghetto Brothers wanted to do it. I said, "I'm sorry, guys. It's not gonna happen. It's not real." I just did that because I was angry.

Every time I went down to Chinatown with my girlfriend, "Yo, Spic!!" "Yo, Chink!" I'm thinking back in retrospect, why did I say that? I'm in their block, in their turf. One time, the same guy walks up to me and I said, "Yo, man, what is your problem with me? Yo, just you and me, alone! You ain't gonna be doing all of that movie stuff, this is for real! I ain't gonna go down to the movies. You and I, without yo boys!" He was like, *Aw*, just looked at me, then he just walked away. 'Cause I mean, these guys were packing. I go back to the Bronx and it still bothered me... I had a Ghetto Brothers division on Henry Street. Right next to Chinatown. But I said, I better not do that because I would jeopardize those Ghetto Brothers.

•••

Everyday could be something crazy in those days, man. You just never knew. Even if you left the Bronx there were problems. You come back to the Bronx, there's more of the same problems waiting for you. There was this time that I went to 14th Street with my boys. So we're down there walking around, hanging out and I said, "Guys, I used to live here on Washington Street. I used to live right here." Every Ghetto Brother that came into the GBs, I introduced them to my family life from when I was a little boy. But this time when we got off the train, and we were walking out through the area, the cops surrounded us. They looked at us and saw our colors: The Bronx?! Ghetto Brothers, the Bronx?! At that time, the Bronx was known for the worst gangs in New York City. The cops said, "huh-uh! You're from the Bronx. Get out!" They escorted us out, from 14th Street to the train station. I said, "Damn, man. Officer, I used to live right here—" "SHUT UP!"

All right. We go to the train station. I said, "GBs, go your way." It was myself, Black Benjie, Louie, and Beast. We're on our way back home, and you know where you transfer to the shuttle on 42nd street, where you change to take the number 2 train? We went there. Black Benjie dropped his helmet in the train tracks. It was a Nazi helmet. Lots of gang members had Nazi helmets and stuff in those days. Real German helmets. Imagine how that made me feel? Me, the secret Jew! So Black Benjie dropped his helmet on the tracks and he went down to get it. I helped him. This Cop said, "Get over here!" I went over to the cop and said, "Officer, you don't wanna do that." He said, "Oh, yeah?" We surrounded him. I said, "You don't wanna do that, right?" He was a rookie cop. And we're just staring at him. He said, "Go on, go on your way." And he walked away. As soon as he did that, we ran. Then he called for backup, but they didn't catch us, cause we saw him getting on his radio. We had already left.

We go back to the block, I go down to 163rd Street. On the top of 163rd Street on Prospect, I was walking. A guy was looking at me. An undercover cop, I didn't know it at the time. I said, "What are you looking at?" He said, "I ain't looking at much." He pushes me. I push him up against the garbage can. He pulls out his badge. As soon as I turn around, two big guys grab me. They take me around Prospect and 163rd Street, throw me inside a building in the basement. And I'm thinking, *They're gonna kill me.*

So the cop comes in and I said, "Man, if you're gonna do something, just do it!" He says, "Oh, you think you're tough?" So he puts his elbow in my neck, and I'm like, *Oh, man!* They started roughing me up. After they roughed me up, they let me go.

I went back to the block. "Yo, Benjy, what happened to you, man?" 'Cause you could see something had happened to me. I said, "It was some cops over here. They're gonna pay for what they did! Big time!" We went up there, looking for them, but they were not around. The next afternoon, some kids were playing at the handball court, Ghetto Brothers turf. The kids came up to me, "Benjy, this cop don't want us to play in the park!" So we surrounded the cop. "Yo! What is your problem?" I said. The cop was like *zip*; he didn't say nothing, totally quiet. I said, "Those kids can play in the park. You don't own anything. Get outta here!" He was like, *That's cool*, and walked away.

The Ghetto Brothers left and he caught me alone. I was going down the block to go home, he stopped me. He grabbed me, kicked me, put his foot up my behind. I was in tears. That hurt so much. When they say a foot up your ass, boy does that hurt! And he hit me, man, and I stood in the corner like, *Oh, my goodness*, that hurt so much!

I waited until the pain went away. I went around 163rd Street and Prospect. I found a huge soda bottle, the old Coca Cola bottle, the hard one, solid like brick. I'm walking down the block, and he's standing near the entrance of the school. He doesn't even notice me. And then as I get close; I can see the whole thing in slow motion. He turns: BOOM!!! Right in his face. I smashed him right in his face with the Coke bottle! And he went like, "UGH!!!" BUHSH!!! The bottle shattered in his face. And I ran.

I came back two, three days later because that was our turf. He wasn't there anymore. A detective walks by, he calls out to me, "Benjy! A cop got hit very seriously with a bottle." "And?!..." I said, like, *Oh, yeah, what you want me to do?* Then I said, "Ghetto Brothers, you know anything about that?" The guys go, "We don't know nothing about that. You know we don't play that, Benjy. We don't be playing that..." "How's the officer?" I said. Cop says, "He's doing very bad. But he's gonna survive this. But we're not going to put him here anymore. Because he's new in this community." Then he said to me, "Benjy, you better not have had anything to do with this." So, they left it at that.

When the cop left, I boasted about what I did to the Ghetto Brothers. "You serious?!" they said. "That's right, man." We went to the spot where the blood was, and you know what happened? I started having feelings of remorse. That wasn't me. I knew inside that wasn't me. I was playing a role I felt that I had to play. It was like two Benjy's. The good one, the one taught by my father; and then there was the bad Benjy, the savage, the gang leader, the one in the street. Looking at that spot where the blood was, I said to myself, *What possessed me to do something like that?* I felt sick in my stomach.

I was playing a role. 'Cause I learned from the streets and watching movies. And I saw John Wayne and the Hell's Angels. So I wanted to do something, play a role to be like them. I wanted to know what it was like to be tough. And I knew that I had to be tough in order to survive in the Bronx.

But being tough comes with consequences. Being the leader of a gang in the Bronx at that time, you know, you're the leader of a bunch of tough guys. Then there's other gangs, too, right? So now what do you have? EVERYBODY'S a tough guy. Everybody's a savage. It was crazy. There was always some kind of war or somebody getting revenge for something somebody did, something some other gang did.

Like with Saint. The guy who stabbed my brother Victor. I wanted to get revenge on him. And my friend

Bodeen, from the Warlocks, comes to me, "Benjy, I can get you Saint! But you gotta kill him!" Before that, we almost had Saint. Saint was the guy we had wanted to get revenge on from earlier — my brother and one of my boys. Saint and the Saints beat up one of my boys, Ape Man! He was a skinny guy, naturally STRONG guy. We saw him walking down the block, and I'm looking at him, he's walking like a zombie. And then he drops. "What happened?" "The Saints beat me up." These were the guys who tried to kill by brother Victor. When Ape Man told me this, I was like, "*What*?!" We knew where The Saints were. So we went to Ghetto Brothers territory. We passed Prospect, all the way to Forest Projects. On our way going to their turf, guess who was in the park? Saint! We saw him. The guys said, "Benjy, there he is!"

We had Saint surrounded in the park this one time. Saint was a black brother. Man, this guy could run. We surrounded him and he escaped. We surrounded this guy, and he just took off! When the guys went to grab him, he went under. And he just took off like a leopard and went down the hill on 163rd Street, yelling, "I'll be back."

I said, "Oh, man!" Some time after that, that's when Bodeen said to me, "Benjy, I'll get him for you. He lives where I live at. But if I get him for you, you gotta kill him!" I said, "O.K., we'll do that."

Two or three days later, it was in the summer, Bodeen brings Saint to the Ghetto Brothers clubhouse. He comes in. We had our colors inside out so he couldn't see who we were, and I was off to the side behind a door, he didn't see me. And I'm looking, and Bodeen says to Saint, "Saint, here's one of your divisions. You didn't know that, but

I helped you put it together." 'Cause Bodeen and Saint knew each other for a long time. Saint said, "Oh, Yeah. That's cool?!"

The Ghetto Brothers clubhouse was divided in two. There was a door here and a door down here. So I come out, like this. I said, "Close the door!" Then I looked at the guys and I went like this, I gave them the kill sign. Remember the old tables in the old days, where you had the leg, the round hard part? One of the GBs broke it off and started to beat Saint. Then all the guys joined in.

Then I walked out. All you heard was screaming. "Aah!!!! Aaaah!!!!" I was outside. They were beating him with table legs, chains, and stuff. They were just doing this guy in. Next thing you know, the door swings wide open. Saint runs out towards me, he's got a knife stuck in his rib. He's grabbing for my leg and he looks up, begging, barely able to talk, "Benjy, Benjy, please don't kill me." He's crawling towards me. And I reach down and hold him up. There was a Ghetto Brother who came out behind him with a fireman's axe. We stole the axe from the fire department. There was constantly fires in the Bronx, so we used to take the axes from the fire department. So this GB is just about to swing and chop this guy up, and I go, "STOP!" He was just about to hit him in the head with the axe.

Man, if you could see how this guy was looking. I said, "Let him go." And he looks at me, and he's just BLEEDING! He's bleeding everywhere. You know the Saigon knives, the ones with the dragon on the side? That was stuck right in his rib. It didn't go between, it hit the bone! So Piano says, "Yo, Benjy, I stabbed this guy!" I was like, "Of course, stupid. But You hit him in the bone!" So Saint gets up while we're talking and he runs down the block. I couldn't believe it. This guy was busted up, man, but somehow, he's able to get up. He's running and I'm looking at him, like this, 'Cause I felt sad for him, man. He asked me not to kill him, "Please…" he said. And I put myself in his shoes. *I don't want this to happen to me*, I thought to myself.

Bodeen goes to me, "You PROMISED!" So, it's like a spirit came over me again. That savage part of me took over. I said, "All right, guys. Go finish the job!" They ran after him. Minutes later, they came back, "He's gone, Benjy." "What happened?" I said. "He split!" So Bodeen goes, "Aw, man…" I said, "Bodeen, don't worry about it, man. You said he lives around your way? Listen, when he gets there, give us a ring. We'll go finish the job." I didn't do it. Two or three days later, I found out Bodeen was killed. "Yo, Benjy," a Savage Nomad said to me, "They killed Bodeen, Benjy." "Who?" I said. "The Saints."

They killed Bodeen. They got him in his basement. One of thes Saints said, "Here," he gave Bodeen a gun, "You're gonna do Russian Roulette." Bodeen said, "How can I do Russian Roulette? This a .45!" I know the story 'Cause one of the Saints told me the whole thing! Now, I'm thinking… Táto, one of my boys said to me, "Damn, Benjy. Even though he was going to die, why couldn't he just shoot them?" It was a psychological thing. He shot himself.

Two or three days later, I'm playing pool with my friend Diego, who's dead now. (Later on, when Diego became a member of the Ghetto Brothers, he started a division of Ghetto Brothers in Chicago. A Mexican gang.) So, I was playing pool with Piano, Táto, and Diego. The door opens. You know when you look in the shadow and you see a lot of heads? I look and I'm like, *OH*!!!! It was Saint! He came to my turf! How did he know? 'Cause none of my boys were there. We had Gestapo. Each gang had their own Gestapo, which were secret guys. "Yo, there not there! They're there alone." He knew when we were alone. Man, when he walks in, and we go like this: just stone, nobody moves. And I'm looking at him, he looked like a mummy 'cause he was all wrapped up with bandages from the hospital.

So we took the pool sticks, and I went, "All right, look. We might die here. But I'm taking somebody!" I was scared. So he looks, turns his head to the side, looks up and he sees our "Rules and Regulations: No weapons" sign on the wall. He says to his boys, "Put your weapons on the table." These guys put EVERYTHING on the table — sawed-off shot guns, .45s, zip guns, knives, everything. Saint walks up to me. Gives me a big hug. "I owe you one, Benjy. You let me live. Whenever you guys need any help, I'll be there for you." Then he walked away. They took their weapons. I stood frozen. Like an hour or two, just standing at the door. When my boys came later on, they were like, "Benjy!" I said, "Yo, guys. We could've been dead right here, right now. Saint came back." "Saint came back?!" "Yeah, he came back! And we're allies now." And I just stood there, staring at the door. I couldn't believe that that happened to me.

You ever seen pictures of werewolves, where the evil comes out of the guy, then it goes back in? Like, the real

Benjy came out, the good Benjy, that's what MayLin, said. "Benjy is not like that. That's a façade. At home, he's no way like that. He likes to clean, he likes to mop, he likes to help me around the house. But when he's out there with those crazy guys and those gangs, Benjy acts that way." That's what it was like for me, like I was a werewolf.

A month later, Saint came to the clubhouse, we got into altercations with the Dirty Dozens. The Dirty Dozens were mobilizing because they had something about us they didn't like. When I looked to the corner, Saint was there with his boys. So, you see what I'm saying? He kept his word. We talked diplomacy. Nothing ever came about because the leader didn't want to fight one on one. His thing was the same philosophy: Everybody all together. So everybody went their own way. I said to myself, *Man, if I keep wearing these colors, I'm gonna have to live this up forever. I don't like this.*

Chapter 6
Running Wild, Stress and Strain

Around the same time that I was starting to feel that way, that I was starting to think about leaving the gang, that's when the killings started piling up. There were killings here, killings there. Hangings, suicides. Junkies being shot at. Prostitutes being raped and murdered. There was no law, everybody was outlaws. The Bronx was just one big deathtrap. The gangs were running rampant. Why? Because the leadership is responsible. The leadership is responsible to tell their boys, "Yo, we're not supposed to do this." But because they wanted to show the world that they were tough, they had to put up an image. So instead of sending out their Presidents to meet the enemy, they would send out their boys. With me, it was the opposite. No matter what was gonna go down, I went out there. I was in the middle of it! I had no choice. This was the time. I was a leader. But leader or not, this is what you had to deal with.

And what's crazy is that, at the height of the gang era, I — my family and me — we were still observing on Fridays! That's why they used to call me "the Preacher." The Ghetto Brothers used to call me the Preacher because I would talk about the Bible to them. I was beginning to know, little by little, what was happening. I started to buy books on Hebrew and Jewish Holidays and everything, and I said, "Aw man, my father does this!" I was beginning to know and understand that I was Jewish. Everything was starting to make sense. All of this was happening right in the middle of the gang era. I was dealing with the gang stuff, all the street stuff and violence and anxiety, all of that; right at the same time I was learning, figuring out who I was, my Jewish faith.

And it all goes back to around when we first moved to the Bronx. When we were younger, we didn't know what those Friday nights were about. We did what we were told, but we knew something was different. Those Friday nights were very important to my father. It wasn't until later on that I learned the truth. That's why we would say, "There's something strange. Why do we do these things?" My brothers and I, we knew we were different from the other Puerto Rican families in the community. At first, no one asked our family nothing.

We asked later. I was the one who asked. When I was eleven years old, after we had moved to the Bronx, I said, "But wait. Why do we do this on Friday night?" And then I asked my father, 'cause he told me that "The Sabbath is God's day, Friday is God's day." I said, "Then why do we go to church on Sunday?" "Shssh! Be quiet." That was his response. He wouldn't talk about it. Always secretive. Any time I asked a question, he was trying to wiggle out of it. He didn't want to tell me. But I was figuring it out. I kept asking him. And much later on, I bought a book called *The Secret Jews*. And everything that it said in there, my father, my parents did the same thing!

I asked my mother, too. I asked my father first. Only later on did I ask my mother. And they both tried to avoid it. My mother would lock herself in the room, quietly put some candles on, and she would start praying. And

I'm looking like this, 'cause she didn't want nobody to see her. Everything was private. It was a private world. Same thing with my father. My father wrapped himself in a white bed sheet. And you'd see him reading with a candle here, a candle here, or a little light. You see him reading the Bible. But there was something about it. I knew something was different. *Moranos*. They didn't want to make a big deal about it. They just didn't want to. They kept it to themselves, because you don't want to get persecuted. The hatred. And there were times that I felt ashamed. Times that I didn't know who I was, or everything that made me who I was. Man, I could not say nothing; I couldn't talk to anybody about it. It was tearing me up inside.

When I was around 13, I asked my father again. I was trying to confirm something, find out who I was. When I asked him, he said, "Just do what I always taught you. That's all that you have to do." And that was it. He was very secretive about the little things he used to do, and nothing was going to change that.

And how did I know which books to check out? It was Rita Fecher. I was talking to Rita Fecher, Manny Dominguez's wife, I asked her questions. She's Jewish. She said, "Benjy, read this book," or "Benjy, read this article, check that out." She suspected that I was trying to tell her something. I would look at her closely. I'd ask her things. You know what she thought in the beginning? Much later on she told me, "Benjy, now that everything's out of the closet, when you used to ask me those things when you were young, I thought that you were an anti-Semite. 'Cause why were you asking me all these questions about being Jewish. *Were you planning to hurt me, were you planning to kill me?* That's what I thought." I said, "No, Rita. I wanted to know who I was."

• • •

You know, for all of the stuff that I've done and seen, I was only arrested a few times. I was able to manage this mostly because I avoided trouble. I use to tell the guys, "Avoid trouble as much as you can. Don't give the cops an excuse to beat you up and arrest you." I was caught breaking lights with Black Benjie. And cops arrested me. I did one day in the Toombs. I felt terrible. So I'm sitting in the jail, and this guy goes, "Yo, man, you in the gangs?" So I'm looking at some of my boys and I'm like, *Oh, my goodness.* My boy Heepo was with me, and my boy Thomas.

There was another time I broke a light; the cops got me in the precinct. My father paid the fine. When we got home, he gave me the whooping of my life!

Then there was this one time, we were on 86th Street in Manhattan. It was three Ghetto Brothers and me. We were looking for something or some place, you know, directions, and I said to this guy, this Italian guy, he was with his woman, "Excuse me, can you give me the direction to…" "Yeah, it's up there!" he said, very rude and tough like, you know. And I said, "Yo, my brother, why do you have to be so stupid, man." Guy says to me, "What did you say?" So we just stood there and then we were just arguing. Two detectives came out of nowhere, a black one and a white one. "Get against the wall!" And I'm like, "We didn't do nothing to this guy." "Get UP AGAINST THE WALL!" the cop yells at me. As soon as we got up against the wall, one of the cops shoots himself in the foot! THE COP SHOT HIMSELF! The gun went off: BOOM!!!! I was like, *Oh, man, what the hell is that?* Then I looked behind me and I see the cop hopping on one foot, the black cop's hopping up and down on one foot. The white detective looked at us and said, "They're going to pin this on you guys." I said, "Come on, man. Officer, don't do it."

So they locked us up. I cried, man. I said, "Can I get a phone call?" I went over to the phone, *"Ghetto Brother!"* one of the cops said, laughing at me, mocking me, making fun of me because I was crying. Remember, we're supposed to be real tough guys in the street, right? But here I am crying in the police precinct like a little girl. I got on the phone, crying, "Mommy, mommy, please help me. Get me out of here." I was crying, that never happened to me. In jail, come on, me? I said, "Mommy, they're accusing me of shooting a cop."

So all of the cops were looking at me while they were finger printing me. One of them says, "Yo, they're gonna put that on you." And right there, I saw the other side of racism, and that's what helped develop more hatred in me towards the cops. And I said to myself, no wonder people hate the cops. The things I've seen on T.V. That poison is in the precinct, too. I said, "Officer, you know I didn't —" "Shut up!" "I didn't do that!" "Yeah? We're going to pin that on you." So they took me down to the Toombs, and after a while, they let me go on bail. They let me go because I didn't have a record.

Next thing, we're gonna go to court. You know what my mother said? She went with me to court, and I said, "There he goes. Mommy, that's the guy who accused me."

The young guy, the Italian guy. My mother said, "Why don't you go to him and ask him to forgive you. You didn't do anything. Oh, come on, humble yourself." So I listened to my mother and I went up to him, the Italian guy. He was there with his father and they were both next to a cop. He was going to testify on the cop's behalf. So I said, "Can I speak to you, please?" He said, "Yeah, what is it?" I said, "Yo, listen, man. You know I asked you for an address, that's it. I just asked you for an address and you know, you got ridiculous with me. And now these cops are claiming that I shot him and that I harassed you. Please don't do this to me, man, I don't want to go to jail." So the guy, he's looking at me closely. Then the cop says to me, "Yo! Mind your business." I said, "I'm talking to him." "Shut up!" The cop says. I said to the Italian guy, "Come on, my brother. Please don't do this to me."

So there was a recess, we go back into court. The judge says to the Italian guy, "You gonna press charges on this guy?" "Nah, I'm not going to do it," he says. Then his father was like, "WHAT?!" He says, "No, dad. He didn't do nothing. I was just angry at my girlfriend at the time. I took it out on him." So the judge says, "That's it?" He said, "Yeah." Then the judge said, "Case closed!" I hugged my mother! I walked up to the Italian guy and I said, "Thank you, brother." He said, "Ah, forget it." And he just walked off. And the cop who saw me that day, he told me, "You're lucky that guy didn't want to press charges on you."

Then the black cop told the truth. He said, "Nah, he didn't shoot me. I shot myself." Truth is, when he put the gun inside the holster, it was cocked and it went off. So they let me go. I told the cop, "Yo, man, thanks a lot, man."

I went back to the block, "Yo, Benjy, what happened?" "Nah, man, I did one day. It was terrible. I wanted to go to the bathroom, but I didn't go." "Why?" "'Cause everybody was looking at me; there's no doors there, guys. You gotta do everything right there."

So, boy, did I learn a lesson that day. And that kept me away even more from not violating the law. Whatever I did, it was all incognito. So I would tell the Ghetto Brothers, "If we're gonna do something, let's do it like the Vietcong."

But jail or not, during this time, when I was flying colors, I did a number of things that I wish I could take back. But there's this one thing that still really stands out to this day. We were on Stebbins Avenue, and I saw two young guys, two Puerto Rican guys, playing in the handball court. I walked over to the handball court and said, "We're gonna play handball." "But we were here first," they said. "SHUT UP! See, now, because you answered me back, now you're going to pay for it." "But why, what did we do?" They were young guys. So I looked at my guys. "To show you that we're bad," that's what I said. The guys were laughing behind me. They beat the hell out of them. Sticks, everything. And these were young guys, no more than 13 years old. And when that was happening, I looked like I was someone else. I went home that day and I was crying. I cried about that, man. I couldn't believe that I did that to those guys. I said to myself, *what possessed me to do that to those two young innocent guys*. Young. It was that evil. The evil Benjy. That wasn't me. Man, that tore me up that I did that to those guys.

About a week later, I go past P.S. 133 and those two young guys were in the school yard. They were bandaged up pretty bad. You could see that they were real banged up. So when I walked up to them they said, "Please, Mr., don't hurt us." I said, "No, no, no... I'm sorry, man. I just want to say that I'm sorry." And these guys had, I mean, SHINERS! Their faces were busted up; we had worked them over pretty bad. I said to myself, *Oh, my goodness.* I told them, "I don't know what to say. I'm sorry, man." They said, "Please, don't hurt us." They were thinking I had come back to kill them or something. And everyone in the school yard had stopped and were looking because there was a lot of us there. So everybody stopped, they were looking, aw, man. The teachers came out, said, "Guys, guys, please. These are young students, don't hurt them." The teachers thought that we were going to beat up everybody. The teachers were scared, too. 'Cause remember, we all had chains and stuff. We looked like a bunch of Hell's Angels. One of the teachers came up to me and said softly, "Guys, please don't do this here." I said, "No, No, we're not here for that. I just came here to talk to these two people."

I turn around and I see the cops! Somebody called the cops, must've been one of the teachers. The cops were all over the place! Detectives walk up. Three detectives were walking up, and the cops were watching and we went up the hill. Me, German, Black Benjie, we go up the hill. I said, "The detectives are coming up the hill. When I say, 'Go,' get out quick." So when the cops were coming, I yelled "Go!" And we took off, and the cops got startled, they were like, *What happened?* They stopped us, "What are you guys doing here? I said, "This is our turf. Like you guys got Fort Apache, that's your turf, this is our turf right here." They let us go, and nothing ever came of that. But what I did to those two young guys haunted me.

So the cops let us go. They understood what I meant about their turf. Fort Apache was an infamous police precinct in the Bronx. They called it Fort Apache, and *we* were supposed to be the savages! They called it Fort Apache because we were supposed to be the Indians — the savages, you know, like the old Western movies? The cops were supposed to be the good guys and we were the bad guys. They were supposed to be the good guys, right? They were supposed to tame the savages — us. They didn't look at us like we were humans. They only saw us as savages. I never forgot this.

I said to this cop, "Fort Apache?" And he said, "Yeah, and you're the savages!" One of the GBs who was there said, "Yo, Benjy, you hear what he said?" I said to the cop, "We're the savages? You're the guys with the guns, not us." They said, "Get outta here." That's why they called it Fort Apache. They were suppose to be the Calvary, and we were the savages. I never forgot that.

Fort Apache was on Simpson Street. It was the 41st Precinct; the 42nd Precinct was on Third Avenue. I lived close to Fort Apache. I lived on Tiffany. Park Street was the next block, at least three blocks from there. Three blocks from where I lived, 'cause I lived at 940 Tiffany. So if you wanted to go to the train station on Simpson that means you have to walk up one long block, make a right, the train station's right there at Simpson, make a left and Fort Apache's right there. I used to say, "This is an insult, my brothers, implying that we're a bunch of savages over here." Now, mind you, *we were trying to be savages;* that's what we were claiming for ourselves; that was part of surviving in the Bronx. You had to be bad, had to be tough. But it was something different about how the cops saw us as savages; they looked at us like we were sub-human. To them, we weren't people, man. Our lives held no value to the cops.

That's when I first started thinking about how much damage we were doing to ourselves, how much damage we were doing to the community. White people didn't throw garbage all over our community. White people weren't responsible for how we were choosing to act. Yeah, there were things done to the Bronx at that time, right. But I was thinking that we still had a responsibility to each other, to the people in our community. And for the first time, that's when I said, "Brothers, we're gonna have to change our image. We're gonna have to prove to the police, we're gonna have to prove to the city government, we're gonna have to prove to the people in this country, that blacks and Puerto Ricans are civilized people, working people. People who love education, people who love their family, who love their children." I wasn't raised the way I had become. My father, my mother, they didn't teach me to become an outlaw. The community was suffering already, and the gangs were making it worse. All of us were guilty of that fact.

I remember speaking to the cop who called us savages, I said to the cop, "Just like in the white community, you got savages. It works both ways, my brother." The cop said, "How do you mean?" "Little Italy," I said to him. "If we walk around there, they'll start beating us up 'cause we don't look like you." The cop just stood there, he didn't say nothing.

You remember the movie *Fort Apache*? Aw, man, there was a big "BOO!!!!" EVERYBODY was booing when Paul Newman came around the South Bronx. At that time he was on Prospect Avenue. Everybody booed him because people were like, "Yo, man, that's not cool." Because there was a part in the movie when the cops were shot and the people came out looking like zombies, and I said to myself, *Man, it looks like they look like they got this part from a zombie movie.* 'Cause nobody does stupid things like that around there. They did this to make us, the people in the South Bronx, look really bad. And people who saw this outside of our community, this is the way they looked at us. This is what the media portrayed what our people were like. And we were nothing of the kind. And then, there was another part in the movie where Paul Newman acted like he was insane and he took his police cap and put it backwards, to disarm this guy. Man, you'd NEVER see a cop do something stupid like that in the South Bronx! You would NEVER see a cop doing something dumb like that. He would've been shot or stabbed doing something stupid like that.

In those days, there was a LOT of hostility between the police and the community because they came into community and, instead of looking out for the people, protecting the people, they terrorized the people. Lots of people didn't trust the police or were scared of them. Listen, in the cops minds they were like, *Look, these guys are gonna kill each other anyway. We might as well sit back, let them kill each other, and then we'll take care of the pieces later on*. When the Ghetto Brothers became a political organization, we didn't allow them to do that because we kept on talking to gang members, "Yo, brothers, be aware. This is what they want us to do. They want us to kill each other. They want us to beat each other up. No, stay alert! And watch what these cops are doing, 'cause these guys are just as bad — even worse — as the gangs around here."

I used to call the cops the Blue Coats. That's what I used to call them. They were just another gang to me. A gang with more guns than everybody. When I was on Channel 5 on "The David Susskind Show" and we were in a discussion, there were many Presidents from different gangs in Channel 5's studios. So David Susskind looked at me and said, "Which is the worst gang in the South Bronx?" I said, "The Blue Coats!" He said, "The Blue Coats? Oh, yeah. Can you describe them to me?" And this guy's an idiot, he didn't pick it up. So I said, "Well, these guys, they all have uniforms, man. They got colors. They got horses. They got cars. And ALL of them got GUNS!" He said, "Oh, my goodness, I mean, aren't the cops going to do anything about them?" I said, "I'm talking about the cops!" And everybody in the studio was laughing.

The cops were terrible; these guys would run up on you, push you up against the wall. And sometimes, you couldn't even look their way. "What are you looking at?" In my case, when I was walking up Prospect Avenue, I just looked at this guy, and he was a cop. I just looked at him and he said, "What are you looking at?" I said, "You." Then he pushed me, then he took me around the corner on Prospect and took me up in this building, with two other officers, and pushed me down the basement. And I thought, I had my colors on, and I said, "But what is your problem? You know? I'm walking down the street, you asked me a question, I gave you a reply. You push me. So what the hell was that about?" You know, I thought they were gonna beat the HELL out of me.

So all of this was weighing on me. It was getting heavy on my heart, my mind, oh, man. I was stressed out. Running a gang, being wild — 'cause I had to be, dealing with the cops, living in a community that looked like a disaster area. All of the poverty, the killings, the junkies. It was all getting to me. It was messing with my mind. Then I started to look at things more closely and I said, "You know, I don't want to do this anymore, man." I started to look at the colors, the cuts and wounds that I had from wars and stuff. I got shot. The stress. The whole thing. I started thinking about how wrong I was. *How wrong it ALL was.* I remember really thinking about that when I got shot.

There was this guy, the guy was not a gang guy, just a guy from the community who didn't like gang guys. So, he wanted to shoot my boy. It was on the corner, on Rogers. This guy wanted to shoot my boy, and I put my boy in back of me. I said, "Oh, yeah. You gonna shoot anybody, right here, my man! Shoot me!" So he shot at me and missed. The bullet ricocheted and hit me. The guy ran. The gun was a .22. Oh, shit, that burns! My boy was like, "Yo, Benjy! You O.K.?" I was like, "It's O.K., it's O.K., it's O.K." I was looking out for my boy. I go to the hospital — my parents didn't know about this — I go to the old Lincoln hospital, and they take care of the wound. They said, "You'll be all right. The bullet just went out, straight through." But if I was to lift it up the skin, you could see a scar.

So that Friday, 'cause I got shot on Monday four days earlier, that Friday, I was in the train station coming down the stairs with one of my boys. And while I'm going down the stairs, I see a guy from the Black Pearls holding one of my boys with a gun to his head. This Black Pearl says, "Yo, Benjy! I'm gonna kill him. I'm gonna kill him, man!" I said, "No, you're not. You're not gonna kill him. And another thing —" "Yo, Benjy, don't say that!" my boy says. I said to the guy, the Black Pearl, "Where you gonna run to?" 'Cause it was me and another GB. Where you gonna run to? "Where you gonna run to, my brother? 'Cause we're gonna catch you anyway." So the guy SQUEEZED THE TRIGGER! Nothing happened. He didn't have no bullets in the gun! He ran; drops the gun. And we picked it up. My boy said, "Yo, Benjy, why you play things like that?" I said, "I took the chance, man. I scared him." My boy started to cry, "Oh, man, I could've been dead." I told him, "Look, I took the chance anyway!" That's who I had become. I had become an outlaw and I took chances like that.

But it was these kind of things that started to bother me. We couldn't go to each other's turf. They could come to our turf, but I couldn't go to their turf. "Nah, you're not allowed to come here, man." "Listen, can we go 'round the store around your way?" "No!" So then, little by little when I started seeing that. It started changing me. And then the wars! The wars were getting worse. EVERYBODY'S flying colors! People getting stabbed, shot, killed. Gang members getting younger, bolder.

I remember the Roman Kings was on 163rd Street, up the block from the Ghetto Brothers headquarters. On Prospect. One day, the leader of the Roman Kings, walks up to me over here from across the street. He walks up to me over here and calls out, "Yo, Benjy." I said, "What's happening?" He says, "I want you to be a witness to this." "What do you want?" I said. I had a judo suit on. All right, so I'm coming out across the street, I didn't know what was going on. So I followed him into this building and we went into this room. Inside, his boys were already holding this guy in there. This Roman King starts talking to the guy, "Ah, 'cause you think you're bad! Our colors look like your colors, and if any of you come through my turf, and remember what you did to me?" BOOM!!!! Sawed off shotgun! He shoots the guy right there! Blew a hole right in the guy's chest! And I'm looking at this with my own eyes.

When I saw that, I was like, "Yo, what the hell are you doing, man?" He says, "Nah, 'cause I wanted to —" "That's not the point. You did it in my turf!" I said. These Roman Kings were young. But they were BAD kids! Their leader couldn't have been no more than 14. Most of them was even younger. The following day, the cops show up at my door, "All right, Benjy, why did you kill that guy?" And the cops already knew my character. I said, "Officer, you know better than that. I didn't do that." The cop said, "All right, give me the name." "I don't know," I said. "I don't know nothing."

So they killed one of the guys. I told the GBs, "We have to start watching the Roman Kings, 'cause these guys are going to get us into trouble." But this was the kind of stuff that was happening in this era. It was normal between the gangs. Everyday some gang was warring with another. Somebody being stabbed, somebody being beaten up, somebody being killed. I wanted to avoid gang fights altogether. I cared for my brothers. I didn't want nothing to happen to them. I was always with my brothers, the Ghetto Brothers, and my flesh and blood brothers. I was just tired. I was split into two Benjy's!

You know, before going home, I would go to my friends house and take a bath or wash up in the street by the fire pump. Then, before going upstairs to my house, I'd take the colors and turn them inside out. I NEVER wanted my father to know what I was doing. Here I am, the leader of one of the biggest gangs in the South Bronx. I'm known all over the streets. *But I was terrified of my father.*

Even when I was in the gang, out in the street, I turned to my father for security. When I was a Ghetto Brother, and I wanted to let my stress out, I would go home, and I had a blanket. And I would just wrap the blanket around me, suck my thumb, and rock back and forth. I used to do that, nobody knows that. And my father used to look at my mother, like, "What's going on?" But that was the child in me. I was stressed out by being in the streets, being the leader of gang, dealing with the gangs. And I found safety in my home. I found peace and security in my father and mother.

When I would come home from dealing with the street and the gang and the other gangs, he would look at me, 'cause he knew something was wrong. He'd have my blanket ready. Because I was his first son. His first son. And I had confidence in him, I trusted my father.

My father wasn't the type to say, "Come here, you know what my son does?" He didn't do things like that. He would never tell your business. He was very quiet. So I used to be with my blanket wrapped around me, with my thumb in my mouth. Me, a GHETTO BROTHER! A real tough guy.

And my brothers, my real brothers, they saw me. They saw me in the corner, but they never said anything, like, "Oh, you know what my brother does?" Even if they were upset with me, they would never say stupid things like that. They knew what I was going through. But I did it, you know what I mean. Aw, man, when I think about that.

So when my father and mother was there, that's what I would do. And you know what I was doing when I did that? I was thinking. Then when I'd get out of that, I became the teenager again, ready to go back on the street and deal with the gangs. 'Cause what I was doing, I was gathering strength to go back out there. I wanted to be hugged, loved, and know that I could turn around and say to myself, *Oh, there goes my father. Oh, there goes my mother.* And I wouldn't be alone or stressed out, and I wouldn't have to act like I wasn't scared.

So most of the time when Ghetto Brothers used to call me, I was STRESSED out, but I couldn't show it. Remember, I had all this stuff going on. I was a gang leader! You have to look at different characters, and you had brothers who thought differently, and you're trying to bring them to a common goal. Even in the Ghetto Brothers I felt alone at times.

See, a leader is like a ship, and on that ship there's the ones that look ahead, looks at his future. I cared for my brothers. If anything was going to happen to them, let it happen to me, that's how I felt. If anything was gonna go down, I thought, let me go try to resolve it before it got out of hand. It's to sit down and say, "You go. You go. You take this gun, you go over there." "Benjy, where you going?" "Don't worry about it. I'm going home." I didn't go home. I went to Savage Skulls territory. I went to Black Spades territory. I went to Bachelor's territory. Taking chances with my own life because I didn't want nothing to happen to my brothers.

So when people from the gang era say to me, "Yo, back in the days, man, we were a family." Yeah, but define it! You came from a broken home to join a gang, and this family is even more destructive than the one you came from. To me, a family meant a mother, a father, shelter, food, love, security. I brought that — that family atmosphere — to the Ghetto Brothers. They even told me that. "Benjy, man, you were treating us like if we're your brothers, man." I was like, "But you *are* my brothers! You are my brothers. I care for you. You know, that's what it comes down to." Unfortunately, I allowed that feeling to leave my heart for some of my brothers. 'Cause I would soon go through a different kind of dark period.

Part 4
Hero

Chapter 7
Poison

The thing about the Ghetto Brothers was we were mostly a fun group to be with. You wanna have fun? You join, you hang out with the Ghetto Brothers. We'd always go down to 14th Street, on the river. And why was it fun? Because we always found entertainment, we always had something to do. That's what we were all about: having fun. But, if you cross the line? If you had a problem with one of us, if you went up against us, that's when you had a problem. But for the most part, we were friends just hanging out, trying to find something to do.

And when I was dealing with all of the gang stuff, I was also trying to read or be around the older the guys, the old men in the community. I always wanted to learn something, and I was very impressionable from a young age. Around this time, at the time of my Puerto Rico nationalist phase, I started becoming a racist. I mean, man, I was learning to be racist; I was being stupid, listening to these racist old Puerto Rican men. I remember, when these things were being taught to me by some of the other older members of the community, the Puerto Rican community. These old guys who used to sit out on the block, playing dominoes, would say, "These young black guys. They're gonna take our Puerto Rican girls." This is what I'm hearing from them. I said, "What?!" They were like, "Yes." So this is what's being fed to me by some of the older men in the Puerto Rican community.

Meanwhile, I'm ignoring what my father taught me and what I know is right. I don't know what I was thinking. I don't make excuses for nothing, you know; I take full responsibility. But with all this gang stuff and stress, I guess it made it easy for me to accept this poison that some of the older men in the community were feeding me.

And it got to a really bad point for me. I remember this one time, I was on 163rd Street and Prospect. I see this beautiful Puerto Rican girl walking around with this black brother. So I stopped them right on the corner and I go like this, "What are you doing around here?" The guy says, "Who are you talking to?" I said, "I'm talking to you." So then, when I was doing this, my hair's standing up on the back of my neck. Some Ghetto Brothers are across the street — we were still a gang at this point. They saw me and they came across the street. "Yo, what's up, Benjy?" It was Beast and them. I said to the girl, "I see this guy walking with you, is that your boyfriend," I asked her in Spanish. She said, "Yes." I told her, "Take your hand away from him," again in Spanish. She motioned to him to leave. Then in Spanish she said, "Depart from this guy." The guy said, "What's happening." I said, "Yo, my man, you see this pole right here?" We were standing right near a light pole. I said, "How would you like to be hung here?" He got in a stance like he was ready to fight. She said to him, "Honey, honey, no. Just go, please, please." He was ready to fight. She stood there. I told her, "You stay. You go!" He says, "Yo, my man, I'll be back!" I told him, "Don't say that. Because if you take the next step and I say the word, you'll never see the light of day again." So she said, "Honey," she was crying, "stop, don't say anything." So the guys were like, "Yo, Benjy, just give us the word. We'll take care of him right now. We'll take him to the basement and just put him away." I said to this guy, "Shut up. Just go!"

After he had left, I took her to this restaurant that was nearby and I said, "Yo, you belong with us. You don't need these guys over here." She said, "But *he's* black," pointing to one of the GBs that was with me. I said, "No, no. But he's *Puerto Rican*. If you wanna go with a black, go out with one of these guys. Go with a Puerto Rican." "But I love him," she said. I felt bad, man. I felt TERRIBLE! 'Cause I never was like that. That wasn't me. What I did that day still hurts my heart. What I said to him? I was ashamed.

See, when that poison, that poison of racism was introduced to me, I didn't analyze it. I just took it for granted. Because what these old bigots told me. I didn't sit down and think, or dismiss them, and all the teachings that my father gave me went out the window. And I kept on doing this. Not so much out in the open at first, but then I started making it known. And then came this time — the most embarrassing moment for me personally and in the history of the Ghetto Brothers. We were about to make war with the Black Spades, and you know what I did? I told all the divisions to get rid of all the blacks. I told them, "I don't want no black Ghetto Brothers to come with us. This is only all Puerto Ricans. We're gonna fight the Spades." Black Ghetto Brothers came to me and said, "Yo, Benjy, man, WE'RE GBs!" "Nah, nah, nah," some other Ghetto Brothers said, some who were also accepting that poison. "You can't trust them, Benjy. 'Cause if we fight with them, they might attack us." So I was like, "Nah, I don't want you guys to go." I told Wayne, he was one of the leaders of a Ghetto Brothers division, "I don't want your boys to be there, we're taking care of this. Just the Puerto Ricans." And then Jimmy comes from New Jersey. Jimmy was the President of the Ghetto Brothers in New Jersey. He comes all the way to the Bronx. He was Puerto Rican. He says to me, "Benjy, what is this I'm hearing? You're getting rid of the blacks in the Ghetto Brothers?" "Yeah," I said, proudly like I was big stuff. "We're going to turn into a nationalist organization." And he looked at me, he was shocked. And one of his main boys who was black was standing right there. I was embarrassed. In my heart, I knew it was wrong. But all of this poison. I let it get to my mind and wipe clean what I know, what my father told me, and what I really feel for all people. I just let that poison wipe away the love I had for my friends. I didn't even think, man. Because of these idiots in the community poisoning my mind.

You know who caught me? My father. You know why? 'Cause Victor and Robert told my father! "Papi, you know what Benjy's doing? He's doing this and saying this about blacks." My father said, "What?!" So my father motioned me over to him. He said, "Get over here. Sit down over here." I was embarrassed and I put my head down. I couldn't face him. I was terrified of my father. My father was so tall, a very strong man, you could feel the aura of his power. And he was a man of wisdom, thoughtful, fair. He looks at me carefully and he says, "So, what is this I'm hearing about you?" I said, "'Cause, the blacks, they start a lot of trouble. You know what I mean. In the park, they start trouble. And they're doing this." And my father cuts me off and says, "And the Puerto Ricans are *innocent*?" "Yeah, but we don't do what they do." "Oh, no? You mean we don't kill. We don't rob? We don't steal? We don't do none of that, right?" So then he started to explain to me when he first came here. "Son, you have no idea what you're talking about." So what was my father doing? He was getting me back to who I really was. "Remember the teachings I taught you? Remember when God said love your neighbor like yourself? Do you think he was just talking about Puerto Ricans? He was talking about all of us. That man is your neighbor. 'Cause if you hate him, then you hate God!" "Pa, I don't hate God—" "THEN YOU DO! Because he made him in his image." And when my father told me that, I was so embarrassed, I felt so bad. I went to my mother's room, my mother looked at me, she said, "We never taught you things like that." She said to me, in Spanish, "Who told you that?" I said, "So and so around the block." "Don't listen to those idiots," she said. "Those guys don't like nobody!"

And tell you how crazy this was, I was with MayLin at the time! She was Chinese. There was a girl named Rose, a Puerto Rican girl, she said, "Benjy, you're a nationalist, man, you're a nationalist. Why don't you drop your girl and come with me?" I said, "I can't do that. She's been with me since day one." We met when we were young. The girl said, "But you're supposed to be a nationalist, stick with your own." She threw it on me, too. And I said, "But I can't do that. I can't do that."

And I was being criticized. "You're saying this about this, but look at your woman. You're saying this about this guy, but your woman ain't Puerto Rican!" I didn't know how to make sense of any of this. I just didn't. I was confused. Because you see, my fear is if you catch me, in a corner, I resort to anger and maybe violence. "Yo, just leave my girlfriend out of this. I don't wanna talk about this. Leave my girl out of this, all right?" "Why? 'Cause you know we're really getting on your nerves speaking the truth to you."

I have to say, though, some Ghetto Brothers, man, really looked out for me. They didn't listen to that nonsense I was saying. They weren't having any of that. Instead of that, they kept all the brothers together. I remember them saying to me, "Yo, Benjy, man, we gotta bring the brothers back together in unity, man. This ain't right!"

What's worse? I was friends with Black Benjie at the time. Black Benjie, from the Savage Nomads. Yo, that was my boy! I loved Black Benjie like my own brother. He used to sleep in my house. But when I was going through this phase, I told myself that he was different. I saw him as a "special" black. And you know how I reasoned that? I said, oh, wait, Black Benjy's from St. Thomas. He's an *island boy*. You see that? See what I did? Oh, I see, he's an island boy. He's like one of us. He's just like us, we're Puerto Rican boys. He comes from the West Indies, so he's acceptable. He never knew that I thought this way at that one time.

And check this out, my brother Victor gets involved with this Puerto Rican girl — a black Puerto Rican. He tells her, "I don't want to introduce you to my brother, Benjy, 'cause he doesn't like blacks. She came up to me one day, and she was like hiding behind my brother Victor.

And I said, "Yo, who is this girl?" "It's my girl, man," my brother said. He just told me straight up, "It's my girl." And I went like this, "Hi, how are you? You're Hispanic?" "Yeah." "Oh, como esta!!!!" So my brother looked. But he didn't understand, he was confused. He didn't know that about me, that I was making special exceptions. "Oh, Benjy, I thought you didn't like —" "No, I said, black Americans. I don't like black Americans. I like black Puerto Ricans." And Victor said, "But, yo, they're the same. They came from the same place!"

See the poison that I'm talking about? They were just old, racist, bigoted men. That's all. They didn't like nobody. I was listening to these idiots! I was young, I was very impressionable. One big mistake — my father taught me, "When people tell you things, Benjy, always have a question mark in your mind. If you're not questioning it and you're accepting it, then you're an idiot!" Now, remember, in those days we were taught to respect our elders. So the old guys used that. They said to me, "Young man, we need people like you to save our community. Look, you see what's happening?" They were feeding me this poison. And instead of following what I knew in my heart and what my father taught me, I listened to these idiots. I let them pollute my mind.

I remember going on Prospect, there was a black owned shop. In those days they were selling the black liberation flag and other similar flags there. So I'm there, I was buying a Puerto Rican flag, and the guy behind the counter says to me, jokingly, "You know, we're going to get all the Puerto Rican girls." All of the Ghetto Brothers were looking at me and I went, "What did you say?! Don't you EVER say that again!" I was dead serious, in a rage. I walked away. My brothers — GBs — were cool guys, and they were like, "Yo, Benjy, man, what the hell is going on with you?" They were all laughing; it was a joke. They got the joke. But I was the only one not laughing.

You see what I'm saying? I was busy listening to these idiot old men on the corner, playing dominoes and talking all of this nonsense. Despite what I knew about my friends, despite my love for my black brothers, I let this poison into my life. And I sat there with these old men, 'cause I used to like to sit around old people and learn, you know. So I said to myself, *They must be right*. I didn't question it, I just said, "Oh, man, really?" to whatever they told me. And they said, "Yes. And if you don't stop them, we're going to lose our language, our culture. They're gonna have a good time with our women and who are we going to be with?" And I said, "Oh, man, that makes a lot of sense." You see how stupid I was. My father didn't teach me that. My father didn't teach me to be foolish. I was always someone with a strong mind, an independent thinker. But at this time, I let that poison in. And then that influence, that poison started to hit me and I started to bring that poison into the Ghetto Brothers, little by little. A few Ghetto Brothers went for that, but the majority of GBs said "NO!"

This created a big problem among the black brothers in the GBs. They came up to me, some of them, "Yo, Benjy, man, you letting us go?" "Nah, nah, because I don't want no problems, man." That's all I said, that's all I kept on saying. MayLin, my ex-wife, was looking at me in disgust. She was disgusted with me. She said, "Where did you get this from?" See, she was another one. She knew that wasn't me. People close to me knew something was going wrong with me. It was that poison.

That poison started making me look different at my black brothers in the Ghetto Brothers. Man, I started going like this, "Yo, man, Charlie, Guys…" "Yeah?" "Take their colors away, I don't want them in here. Tell 'em to go join another club. The Black Pearls or The Black Spades." But guess what? Word never got to them. They never told them that I said that. So here I am thinking they told them what I said.

Then we were going to have this big fight with the Saints, and I remember Wayne, a very good friend, came up to me. He was the President of one of the Ghetto Brothers divisions, one of my very strong divisions from Morris High School. And when we're fighting with The Saints, and I looked to my right and I see all these guys, all these black brothers. I said, "We were surrounded!" He said, "No, Benjy, those are Ghetto Brothers!"

So when Wayne said to me, "Benjy, we played together for many years. I went to your house, I ate over there. Why you doing this, man?" "Nah, 'cause I don't want no problems." "What-a-you-mean, PROBLEMS? We're all Ghetto Brothers." "Nah, I don't know." I couldn't look him in his face. Then when I did look him straight in his face, I wanted to cry. That was my brother. I had to fight back my tears, man. I knew I was wrong, I felt in my heart, in my bones. But that poison, man. Wayne said, "Look, Benjy. I'm gonna stick with the GBs, man. We're not going. 'Cause we did some good stuff." Then later, that's when my father approached me; my brothers opened their mouths to my family.

During this period, I was still struggling with two Benjy's. There was, on one hand, the real Benjy, and on the other hand, there was the evil Benjy. The streets, the poverty, the fires, the abandoned buildings, the gangs, the stress — all of that created the evil Benjy. And the influence of the old, bigoted, stupid, idiots in the Puerto Rican community just made me even worse.

And during my racist days, I met the Hell's Angels, again. When I went to the block, after that introduction, when I was told, "You're old enough to die." I remember a week after that, Big John, one of the Hell's Angels was on a bike, big 3-wheeler. I'm walking down the block with some Ghetto Brothers, "Hey, Benjy?" the Hell's Angel yelled, "Today is Get-a-Nigger Day!" I said, "Why?" "We're gonna go down to Delancey and we're gonna grab a nigger and beat the hell out of him." "Why?" "Because they beat up one of our boys. You wanna come with us?" I said to him, "I can't do that 'cause we have allies." He said, "O.K., we'll take care of business."

I never forgot that. So one day, I walked up to Sandy, I said, "Sandy, I wanna be a Hell's Angel. Are there any blacks in the Hell's Angels?" "Nope. You see any? Nah, we don't have any. In the Hell's Angels? We don't have blacks in the Hell's Angels." I took that to mean like — it confirmed what those old Puerto Rican guys told me. So I thought to myself, *Aw, man it's better to be like this.* And I see all these three Hs. I wanted it like THIS. I still wanted to be a real tough guy. But it didn't fit because I lived among blacks. I lived among my brothers and the people. And Black Benjie, from the Savage Nomads, which I never told him. If I would have said that to Black

Benjie, he probably would've cried or something. 'Cause MayLin used to tell me, "How are you gonna think like that, you idiot? When your friend Black Benjie's right there?" "Don't say nothing?" "Oh, yeah?! You keep it up, I'm gonna tell him." "Oh, oh, MayLin, please don't say nothing." This compounded everything. The GANG stuff. This poison. My goodness.

Then the poison left me. It never really took complete hold over me anyway. I was impressionable and I was being stupid. It hurt my heart that whole time. This whole time, I didn't even feel right. Then I came back to who I really was, and I told the Ghetto Brothers, "I wanna bring the Ghetto Brothers back together in unity." I remember when I did that, my sister wrote a beautiful poem about me. She wrote that poem right after I said, "I wanna bring the Ghetto Brothers back together in unity." You know what my sister said? She said, "I love my brother, 'cause my brother's not a racist." She's writing this, and I said, "Why'd you write this?" She said, "Benjy, 'cause I never knew you for that. That ain't you."

•••

Around the same time I was getting over suffering from the poison of racism, my understanding of a different kind of poison, the poison of dope, started to grow in the Bronx. My brother Victor was the one who first taught me about dope. "Yo, Benjy, this is dope. This is what dope does to you!" he said. Before that, I had no idea about dope. I was ignorant to the fact. My brother Victor was shooting up drugs from the beginning, '69/'70. But I had NO idea. At that time, the Bronx was full of drugs! My brother was experimenting with this. And the guy took LSD. He took acid. And Robert, too. But Robert never took dope, heroin. My brother Victor did.

Victor was strung out on dope. You know, I really feel sad for my brother. All that time, my brothers would talk to each other. Victor would say to Robert, "Yo, I'm gonna tell Benjy, man. 'Cause he doesn't want drugs in the Ghetto Brothers club." So Victor was the one who taught me about dope. All this time I'm thinking, when I see this brother over here, Charlie, and he looks tired and all. Victor says to me, "Benjy, he's high on dope!"

In those days, my mind was set on the community. I didn't know too much about the drugs in early 1971. I remember things started to change. When I came back to the Ghetto Brothers again, after that situation with my brother and the guy he killed and I started the GBs again. But this time, by 1971, I was moving the Ghetto Brothers into the direction of a political organization. So I finally laid back and started to notice things much more clearly, and I see Charlie constantly nodding off, constantly. I thought he was just sleepy all the time.

I would say to Victor, "How can Charlie stand up and go all the way down like that?" "Look, Benjy, I know that you and Charlie are close, and you love him and everything like that. But, he's using drugs." So, in other words, he lied to me. Charlie lied to me, he hid the fact from me. I said, "Victor, what's up?" Victor said, "I use dope, too, Benjy."

I remember the first time I saw the needle marks on Victor's arm. I cried. 'Cause I never knew. When the drug situation, the epidemic, I never conceived, I could never believe that my own brother was involved with this. And

I cried, "Aw, Victor, man, how could you do this?" "Aw, you know, that's the way it is, Benjy, man. You see, you talking about these people, but I'm one of them, too." And he taught me everything, from the music even to that. I said, "What?! Man…" And I remember Victor saying, "Yeah, man, you didn't see me all skinny," and he talked like that with a bit of slur. "Ay, yo, that's what we do, man. We go into the buildings and we do this. That's why when we used to do it, we did it when you wasn't around." So now he's educated me. Drug dealers?! I'm thinking aspirin!

That was my introduction to drugs. That was my introduction to an education on a lot of different things. My eyes were opening. I'm in the midst of fire. I'm in the midst of violence. I'm in the midst of deterioration. I'm in the midst of government corruption. Oppression. Police brutality. But Drugs? Man, that didn't even cross my mind. I didn't know what it was.

I was *cacero*. The word *cacero* in Spanish means one who is always at home. So I was with the Ghetto Brothers all the time. But afterwards, a lot of times I just went home to think and rest, get my mind right just to go back out there in the street. I just sat down. Close to my father, with my mother. I was sitting down, looking at T.V. The only time I liked to go out was during the evening. Let me go to the block, see what's happening around the block. So that — the drug world — did not exist for me. When Victor opened my eyes that year and he said, "Benjy, that's why you see a lot of people in the street nodding all over the place. That's called dope."

Victor actually showed me how it was done, step by step. First, he started to cook the dope, the heroin, he started to cook it up. He said, "See, Benjy, this is the cooker." He took a cap, a bottle cap. It was a glass bottle. The old Coca Cola bottle cap. That little cap. Then he put some white powder in there. "So, here's what you do, Benjy. And then you cook it. And then it turns like liquid. Then you take the needle." This is what I saw. He did everything right in front of me. And then the powder turned into liquid. Then he pulled the dope into the needle. Then he took his belt and strapped it around his arm and tied it. And I'm looking at this, like, *What?!* And I saw the vein in his arm stand out. And he hits it. I said, "Victor, where'd you learn that?" "Don't worry about that. Don't worry about that!" he says. I couldn't believe what I was seeing. My own brother shooting up dope.

This was out in the street, in an apartment in one of the abandon buildings. "See, Benjy. Look at the floor." I looked down and was like, "OH!!!!" I see all these used needles on the floor. There were needles everywhere. He said, "This is what dope addicts do! They come to these buildings." And he said, "Benjy, you gotta be careful. Because when they want something, they're gonna steal."

Now, a dope addict really doesn't go around hurting people. Dope addicts in those days, their thing was, just go to your house, be friends with you, maybe steal things. Victor said, "Their thing was stealing, they don't bother you. But that's to support their habit. As opposed to me. See, I support my habit. But then, if I couldn't support my habit, then I'd steal." He even would steal from our house. This blew my mind.

That tells you something. That I was very ignorant — in the beginning — when it came to the drug epidemic in the Bronx. 'Cause I wasn't into drugs. That was not my scene. That didn't even bother me. It didn't phase me. I didn't even want to experiment with that stuff. To me, that meant nothing. But to my brother? Oh, my goodness. When I saw him constantly nodding. And I'd say, "Yo, Robert, what's happened to him?" "Ah, he's tired." Meanwhile, that's what it was: He was shooting up dope!

I knew there was a drug epidemic in the Bronx right after my brother Victor told me that. I started to read, I started to open up my eyes, I started to ask questions. And when I started asking questions, when I started realizing the drug epidemic, it was right after we'd just began the transformation of the Ghetto Brothers from the gang to the political organization. This was the middle of 1971.

Now, remember, at this time I'm over here, doing this and doing that for the community. I wasn't looking at the overall picture yet. My brother Victor was thinking that Robert and I would never do drugs. So, one day, Victor looked at Robert and said, "Yo! Don't protect him, man. Let him know. Let Benjy know this is the real thing." So when Victor said, "Yo, Benjy. There's dope everywhere. You see that guy over there?" "Yeah." "That guy's selling dope." "And you see that guy over there? That guy's selling dope. You see this guy over here? This guy's selling LSD." And then I started to really open my eyes, because my concern was cleaning up the community. I was already thinking about how to help change things, right when I learned about this drug epidemic; something that was just as bad, if not worse, than the gangs and the cops and everything else.

My transformation was taking place. I was already cracking from the pressure and strain of the gang. I was stressed out. And I started to feel good again when I started turning my attention to helping the community. That's when I started feeling good, when I started focusing my attention on helping the community. I wasn't feeling bad anymore on the inside. That other Benjy was leaving me. My concern was now on things like helping the people in the buildings that didn't have heat. Helping the people that were hungry. Helping the people that didn't have clothes. But I got zombies walking around here! That's when Victor started to say, "This is called dope, Benjy! Just go into the abandoned buildings and you see guys using dope in there." That's when later on, I started to walk up to the drug dealers and say, "Yo, my brothers, you can't sell this here. You gotta go somewhere else."

It blew me away. It was a lot for me to take all at once. First, that there was this drug epidemic going on. But then second, that my brother Victor was using dope, too. I looked up to Victor. He was the one that taught me so much. Even though he was my younger brother, he taught me a lot. But the drug scene, that was never a part of my life at that time, 'cause I didn't open up my eyes in this area. And then when I finally started to look around, I said, "Oh, my goodness! This is all over the place!" When I saw people nodding everywhere, I remembered what Victor told me. And I thought: *So that's what dope does. It's killing these brothers and sisters. It's destroying people.* Nobody goes to school. People are robbing and stealing. People robbed. People robbed to support their habit! They steal. They shoot. They stab. If you can't work for it, then you have to get it someway.

In those days, I, personally, don't remember any gangs selling dope. And I'm sure, looking in retrospect, I'm sure that they probably were. Because a lot of these guys were getting money from somewhere. Remember, a lot of these guys in the gangs bought serious weapons. You know, so, in order for you to have money for the kind of weapons they had, you got to sell something. You gotta be getting some real money from somewhere. So looking back then, I'm saying to myself, *No wonder a lot of these gangs were buying guns and stuff. 'Cause they were selling this crap.* Looking back, it was really sad, man.

It goes to show that I lived in two worlds. I lived in a world of ignorance, or maybe I didn't want to see it. That's when I started to mobilize the Ghetto Brothers, I said, "Yo! We gotta get rid of this man. We gotta get rid of the drugs. See, that guy over there? We gotta get him outta there. No violence. Just walk up to him and say, 'Yo! You gotta go somewhere else.'"

This is also when Victor told me that he wanted to stop using dope. He wanted to stop cold turkey. I never knew the expression, "cold turkey." "Victor, what is that? What is cold turkey?" I was asking about a GB who was doing dope. He had said that he wanted to go Cold Turkey. Victor said, "He wants to stop dope." "But what does that mean?" "That means he wants to stop completely. And fast!" So, you know what we did? We locked him up in the Ghetto Brothers clubhouse. And when he stayed there, he stayed with my brother Victor. And there was another guy named Louie who stayed with him while he was vomiting and going through a lot of changes to stop using dope.

That's when I declared war on drugs. Why? Because my brother Victor made me aware. He said, "Benjy, if you don't get this out of the community, it's going to kill our young people. If you don't get this out of the community, our young people are going to die. 'Cause that's our future." "So, how do we do it?" I said. "See, the drug pushers?" "Yeah." "That's just another part of the story. Gotta get these guys outta here. But you gotta remember, Benjy, there are gang members — not gangs, members — that are being paid off." "What do you mean, 'paid off?'"

I found out that there were members of clubs that were being paid off by the police to bring in drugs to destroy the community and to destroy the gangs also. And sometimes, they would pay them to get rid of gang members, or leaders — people like me! And sometimes the drug dealers would pay some gang members, you know, to protect them —"Yo, man, I'll give you this and this if you be looking out for me." And by "looking out for me," you know what they were specifically talking about? Ghetto Brothers! They wanted us gone. So after dealing with all of the gang stuff, building up one reputation, after the transformation we were getting another reputation for wanting to help the community. Which meant we were a target for those who didn't want to see things in the community cleaned up. Drug dealers were making money; some cops were making money; some gangs were making money. They didn't like the Ghetto Brothers' new message of peace and cleaning up the community.

In the original Ghetto Brothers "Rules and Regulations" it says, "No drugs in the Ghetto Brothers." The guys asked me, "Benjy, how are we going to deal with these drugs?" First thing I said, "Number 1, these are our brothers, we will not harm them. 'Cause then we will just be compounding the problem. We have to be able to get to the source of the problem that we know is coming from outside." We knew that it was coming from an outside source, coming into our community. I realized something: *They wanna kill our people*! And they're doing it through drugs, bad diet, bad education, bad housing, bad social services. So the drugs were just another step to killing us all off.

From the beginning of '71 to the end of '71, that whole year, that was my education about the drug epidemic in the Bronx. We went to a drug rehabilitation center. What we got? Paraphernalia. Then, United Bronx Parents played a very crucial role. United Bronx Parents was not a drug rehabilitation center, but they had connections with those people. So what those counselors would do is, they would provide us with the literature. We give it to the Ghetto Brothers. The Ghetto Brothers would get it to the community. And then my brother Victor was my scout. "Victor, can you do me a favor? Can you spot GBs who are doing dope?" "I'll let you know what Ghetto Brothers are doing it, Benjy. Right there!" "What?!"

My approach to a GB after I found out that they were doing dope would be this. I would sit down with him. And my brother Victor would be right here. So when I'm asking questions, Victor would say, "Be honest, my brother." Because Victor already knew. One time, this GB started to cry, he said, "I did, Benjy." "No! I never knew that you would use something like that," I said. "Yo, Benjy, I need help." "That's what we're here for, man. That's why we're here." So you know what we did? We locked him up along with other GBs who were using dope, in the Ghetto Brothers clubhouse with ex-Ghetto Brothers that my brother knew. Victor didn't want to be there. He said, "See, Benjy. If they want help, they do it. He just said he needs help." We put them in the Ghetto Brothers clubhouse. We locked the two doors on two sides; and the only ones that were there were those who wanted to go cold turkey. Guys were vomiting all over the place.

The Ghetto Brothers who were there — the veterans — they would take care of these guys. Man, I did this because I cared for my brothers. I wanted to help them get clean. I didn't want to see anybody on dope, especially my brothers. Dope is a poison.

From there, we started to branch out, not only for Ghetto Brothers. We started going up to brothers who were getting high. "Yo, brothers, listen. Man, you don't need to be like this." At this point, I was now fully committed to helping the community in any way that I could.

Chapter 8
It's Not About Colors Anymore

We were sitting upstairs in the living room on 940 Tiffany. Me, Victor, and Robert. I'm in deep thought. I'm calm, and I feel good, and Robert says to me, "Yo, Benjy, what are you going to do, my brother?" I said, "You know, I'm thinking." Remember, I didn't talk to my boys about everything, I talked to my real brothers about everything I was thinking. I said to them, "I'm thinking about changing this." "What'you wanna do, man?" Robert says. I said, "I wanna become an organization. I'm tired of this crap. Hurting people. Stabbing people. You think I want to be bad, you know what I mean? I'm sick of walking around, intimidating people, looking for trouble, worrying about being killed. You think I want all of that?"

It was around this time that I first started to open my eyes. When we were in the Savage Nomads, and we saw the Black Panthers and the Young Lords, that's actually what the political organization form of the Ghetto Brothers was first inspired by. I was inspired by that. I had always been curious. I had always been about learning, reading. I was really interested in history. And those organizations and other people helped inspire me to learn more Puerto Rican, Spanish, and African history.

I was really into history. I read and I learned a lot, I listened to people who shared my interest for history. History was my thing. I knew a lot of different historical stuff about culture that most people didn't know or even care about. For instance, when the Spanish first came into Puerto Rico, there were 30,000 Taino Indians in the island. The Dominican Republic had 100,000 of the same people, same tribes. But when the Spanish went in there, many of the Indians died of diseases. Some of them intermarried. And the rest escaped to other islands. In 1511, the Spanish brought Africans. What the Spanish noticed about the Africans was that they were stronger than the Indians they reported to. Isn't that embarrassing? Think about that. When I was talking to some Mexicans, they were telling me about the Aztecs; the powerful Aztecs and the Incas! Yeah, but the Africans outlived them. The Spanish brought the Africans to finish the job the Indians couldn't do! When the Spanish put all the heavy labor on the Indians, they died off. The Africans developed more power. That's why they were known as powerful people. You could put them anywhere. In the winter or in June, and they stayed strong. My father said, "They're very strong people." So that's well respected.

And you know Arroz con Pollo — rice with chicken? The famous rice with chicken that's in every Puerto Rican and Dominican restaurant in New York City? In Puerto Rico, they teach you this: That's an African plate. The teachers would say this. The Spaniards would give the slaves rice, "Here you go." The Africans looked, took the chicken. Here's what the Spanish would do. They would observe the Africans and write everything down. They saw the Africans take the chicken, pluck it, cut off the head, empty out the blood. This is what the Spaniards seeing. The Africans cooked it, put it together, and the Spanish called it Arroz con Pollo — Chicken with Rice!

The Africans introduced that to the Puerto Rican cuisine and culture. Isn't that interesting?

The Americans came into Puerto Rico in 1898. Remember, they already got Cuba, now they're coming into Puerto Rico. In 1898, the Spanish-American War, Americans invaded Puerto Rico. And there was a famous black man in Puerto Rican history. He stood up against the Americans with all the Puerto Ricans here. They shot his arm off and he was still fighting! He was like, "Nah, I'm not going. This is my country. If you're gonna take us, hell, you're gonna have to kill us." But remember, the Americans had an overwhelming force. They had better ships and everything. Spain was already going down the drain.

So from July 25th, 1898, from that time on, they stayed to this very day. And Puerto Rico became a commonwealth later on. Why? Because look at where the island is situated. The island is here. Europe is over here. Africa is over here. South America is over here. So any enemy ship that's coming from here, you're gonna have to pass Puerto Rico. That's why they got the biggest radar over there. So Puerto Rico is like a military instillation. They could see the enemy coming from miles. During the Nazi era, Germany, they prowled Puerto Rican waters. Remember, 'cause it was American territory, and the Americans would see them. You see what I'm saying?

So when you go to Puerto Rico, you see people of different shades and colors. You have the Dutch, the French, the British, the Africans. Remember, during the wars of Haiti? Many Haitians went to Puerto Rico during the war for independence. When all the South American countries come for their independence from Spain, most of the Spanish went to Puerto Rico. Because it was the last Spanish bastion. I was born in that old city, San Juan.

San Juan was named after St. John the Baptist. It was the opposite, though. Originally, the whole island was called San Juan and the capitol city was called Puerto Rico. But the Spanish turned it around and changed San Juan to the capitol and called Puerto Rico the island. So San Juan was named after St. John the Baptist, Jesus' cousin. That's why, look, the shield of Puerto Rico has a bible with a little lamb, and then in Latin on the bottom it says, "John is his name." So they called the island after John the Baptist.

You know who introduced me to all of this history? It was a black man! I was in Chinatown waiting for MayLin. This black brother passes by and he hears me saying, "Man, these Chinese are something else." He says, "Hey, yo, my brother! You know that Puerto Rico has a history, too?" I said, "What you mean?" He said, "Yo, my brother, before Jamestown in this country was put up, San Juan, the port of San Juan, was already there 400 years. So while the Americans had their little Pilgrims here, you people already had a port. My brother, Puerto Rico was already an established city way before Jamestown. While they were having log cabins, you people had city walls. You were stopping the British. You were stopping the French. You were stopping the Dutch." I said, "That little Island?" He said, "Yes! Read about it!" And he looked at me and just walked away. When my wife, who was my girlfriend at the time, came I said, "MayLin, you know what that guy said to me?" This guy really knew his stuff. He encouraged me. I was 18 at the time. He introduced me to it. And from that point, I started to read Puerto Rican history and other history, too. It was that black brother who inspired me.

At this point, I was always in the library. I brought tons of books to my house. Going to the library and I'm seeing all of this information, it made me start buying books. I forgot this guy's name who introduced me to this world, but it was him who really introduced me to books and a love for history. This was also when that poison of racism started to leave me and when I returned to who I really was.

You know what? I was the type, and I still am, that if you introduced me to something, I wanted to look into it. But it was the way that first brother said it to me, "You know, brother, Spanish is not the only ones who got history. You better start getting into your own. Africa got history. All these countries, every country. God doesn't let nothing pass by. Everybody has contributed something to society. So don't let this guy over here tell you, 'Oh, I'm an American. I've been here in America…' You tell him, 'That little island, before you was here, we were already here!'"

He was the first guy to correct me on Christopher Columbus. He said, "Brother, did you know that the first man to set foot in the United States from the European side was not Christopher Columbus. It was Ponce de Leon." I said, "But I was always told that it was Columbus who discovered America?" "He never set foot in the United States. It was in South America he stepped foot in. When he say he discovered America, he didn't know what he was talking about. And you can't discover a place where people are already living with their own culture. But the one who stepped foot in Florida was Ponce de Leon."

The Spanish came with black men, African men. Now, remember, they became Christianized, so they called them Spanish names. So when an African becomes a Christian, they call him a Spanish name. And there was a certain African. He was in the United States with the Spaniards. And he walked, long distances in Florida, all the way down on the coastal side of the United States. First man, was a black man. And he had a Spanish name because he was a Christian. Remember, when you become a Muslim, they give you a Muslim name. But he lived in Spain, he became Christianized, and they gave him a Spanish name, and he was Don, whatever his name was, and he walked all those areas on foot. That's what my father said. "You see, that's fortitude!" He said, "That's why the African people, Puerto Rican people are very strong people. And they're very clannish."

When the 65th Regiment, the famous 65th Regiment of Puerto Rico, went to the South and the whites saw the black Puerto Rican, the white Puerto Ricans surrounded him. And the white southerners started asking, "What is he doing here?" The white Puerto Ricans said, "He's one of us." The American mind couldn't understand that. Why is a white Puerto Rican, blue eyed, blond hair saying that he's one of you. The white men, they couldn't understand that.

Remember Malcolm X. He made a point: *Isn't it interesting how this country is. Here you got Africans and then the President of the United States told these Klansmen, 'Don't touch these guys, these are Africans.' When they see them, they don't touch them. But when they see black Americans, they hurt them.* He said, "That doesn't make any sense." When the brothers came from the same root. And I'm taking all of this in. I'm learning, thinking about what my father told me about people.

Remember Schomburg? Now, you know Arturo Alfonso Schomburg is Puerto Rican. He contributed much to African-American/Black American history. I was at the Schomburg Center one time and his sons were speaking, they remembered a story about their father. They said, "My father was of Puerto Rican independence. The cops caught my father in the South while he was driving in a car. 'Get out the car!' Remember, he was a black Puerto-Rican. He showed his I.D. 'Born in Puerto Rico. All right. Let him go.'" I asked Schomburg's son, "Why did they do that?" He said, "You have to understand, Benjamin, back in the day at that time, this country was a very hypocritical country. They knew my father was black. But he was not a black American! He was a black Puerto Rican. Way different culture."

Around this time is when I started reading the biography of Malcolm X. He explained it in there. That's why he also called this nation a hypocritical nation. That you would allow this man to hang this man, but you couldn't touch this man because he's African. *Brother, this man came from the same place he came from.*

You know what my father said about the hair? One day, when I was a young boy, I said, "Pa, they're saying that black people have bad hair." My father said, "Bad hair? You wanna know what bad hair is? Come over here. Sit down! Look at that derelict." He pointed to a white man with straight hair. "Look over there. You see that bum?! That man's got bad hair. He doesn't take a bath. He doesn't keep his hair combed, well groomed. He's got bugs in his hair. THAT'S bad hair." You get what my father was saying? A man who takes care of his hair. And then my father points to a black man. Remember, in the old days? Afro Sheen? My father said, "Now, look at this man." He pointed to a black man with a well-kept afro. "Look at this man. He's well-shaven. His puffy hair is nice and shiny. That's good hair!" So what did my father teach me that day? Not to think like everybody else. He said, "Son, look at these flowers. See the beauty of the different colors of the flowers. If you can say that they're beautiful and you can behold the beauty of a flower, why do you think when God made men of different shades — Chinese, black men, Indian — that you can say, 'That's beautiful?'"

My reading, learning, talking to knowledgeable people, cured me of the poison, that brief period of racism I went through. I started to feel good about myself again because I was being who I was. I was never really racist, I was just listening to those idiot people, and I let them get into my mind. My father taught me well. I knew better. That's what brought me back to who I really was.

•••

Even though all the gangs were warring with each other, one thing I gotta say is, there was a lot of mixing of the races and groups. What's interesting about when we lived in the South Bronx is that we all were neighbors. We all went to the same schools. We all lived and breathed in the same place. When they — the blacks — had jobs, they had summer jobs, we were all there, too. When we all went to the park to play baseball, handball, basketball, they were all there. So these are our brothers! So we grew up together in this community. Remember, in the Puerto Rican community, Puerto Ricans come in various colors. You got black Puerto Ricans, white Puerto Ricans.

So when we see brothers coming from the South, the Southern part of the U.S., we understand that. 'Cause you had people who came from the South during the early '70s up to the South Bronx. "Yo, were you from, man?" "I'm from South Carolina." "Where you from?" "I'm from Alabama." You know what I mean.

For us to be together, as a group, we had to stick together. But then you know what I started to notice? I noticed that our peoples live in certain communities. You can tell a black community, you can tell a Puerto Rican community. Most of the Puerto Ricans lived on avenues. All the stores. And a lot of the black brothers we knew lived on intervals. The middle blocks; most blacks lived there. When you said, Union and Tiffany, you knew that most of the blacks lived there. Why? When you looked at that part, that was their block. That was their community. When you come up 'round the way, you hear the bop doo doo doo bop! That kind of singing, and the music. Then over here, oh, there goes the Puerto Ricans playing dominoes in the street. So you could tell what block you were on. Every block was alive with its own distinct culture within a culture.

But the thing about it, everything was done with caution. If you're gonna go to this block, you gotta go with a person that knows somebody from over there. You couldn't just walk through any block. If you didn't know anybody on that block, it could be trouble. You roll up on a block and people would be like, "Yo, my man, can I help you?!" "I'm going to see Clarence." "Oh, you know Clarence?" "Yeah, yeah, we go to the same school." You see what I'm saying?

Racial divisions in our community in the Bronx was different. Even when I lived on Washington Street and Horatio, the Italians were on 10th Street, the Irish were on Hudson, the Puerto Ricans were right in the middle. So when we moved to the Bronx and we went to school, I noticed the same type of thing. When we looked at Tiffany Street and we said, this is their community, this is the blacks' community. Like, "Look, they mostly live here." So we already know, let's keep cool. This is their turf. When they came around our way, they knew: All these are Puerto Ricans that live over here. It was never like, "Get away from here." It was just that certain look, like, "What are you coming around here for?"

But the gangs changed a lot of that, BIG TIME! When the gangs started to emerge as brothers, it changed a lot of that racial division stuff. That's when the guys from Tiffany started joining these guys over here. The guys from here started to join the brothers there. Black Spades (who were mostly in the projects). Who was it that also joined them? Puerto Ricans that were living right there. The Black Spades had Puerto Ricans, too. Plus, those guys were smart. *I'm not gonna leave Puerto Ricans out. You think I'm just gonna have an all black gang? When I can use these brothers too? 'Cause I can use the Puerto Ricans as spies. You know, to go into a Puerto Rican neighborhood.* So race was really no thing for most people. It's just some old Puerto Rican guys didn't want mixing. But that's stupid. We were all one community; we were all in the same boat mixing anyway. The gangs really manifested that and reflected what the community was *really* like.

And my concern for the community had started to grow. What started it was, when I started watching the television, seeing what was happening in California with the Black Panthers. When I started seeing that and I said, what is going on over here? I see posters, police brutality. I see water hoses. I see dogs. I said, "Oh, my goodness. In America? Ah, that could never happen in New York."

When I saw what was going on in California, at that time I thought the Bronx was better, I thought the conditions in the Bronx were better. With all of the poverty, violence, and drugs in the Bronx, I thought the Bronx was still better just because it didn't have all that stuff with the water hoses and the police brutality. We had police brutality in the Bronx, for sure. But not what I was seeing on television with the Black Panthers in California. So you know the expression, "That's over there, it would never happen over here." *The cops are a little more sophisticated, the people here are cool,* this is what I'm thinking to myself. Not realizing that the cops in the Bronx were just as bad, or that people are people. Color is still color. Hate is still hate. Racism is still racism.

But that stuff did come to New York, and for the first time, when I'm on Prospect Ave with my brothers and I'm looking, and I saw cops with helmets, which I've never seen before. And I said, "Yo, what's with the helmets, man?" It looked like these guys were ready for war. So my friend, Sly, a black brother, he said, "Benjy, you see those guys? Those are riot cops." "Riot cops?!" I had never heard that term before in my life. "Yeah, oh, man, if you do something, they're going to hit you upside your head." So then, all of sudden, you had this fear. "Oh, my goodness. You mean to tell me they're gonna come to my house?" "No, no, they don't do that, man. Just what you do is, don't stare at them!" That's what I was always told. "Don't look at them bad. And don't stare at them!" Because they always had the sticks ready.

But then I started seeing stuff. I'll never forgot this. It was on Webster Avenue where I saw a cop in the projects hit a young black boy in the leg and hit him right in the head with his nightstick. A young boy, the cop hit him right on the forehead, cracked his head wide open. And I saw the little boy screaming, and I'm looking, and I yelled at the cop, "Why'd you hit him?" And the cop swung at ME! We all started to run. You get what I'm saying? The cop didn't see any difference between me and the young black brother. See what I mean? The cop tried to hit me, too! I was with the Ghetto Brothers — GBs. It was in early '71, right before we started the transition to the Ghetto Brothers organization. And I started to look and I said, "Yo, I didn't like that guy actually swinging." And one of the GBs I was with said, "Yo, Benjy, man, you saw what that cop did to that little boy? It was like the cop was trying to kill that little boy."

So I was already thinking war; I was already thinking war against the cops. I said, "Listen, we gotta defend ourselves against the blue coats. I told the Ghetto Brothers, let's get together, I want a meeting. Then little by little, as time went on, the organizations were coming up, like United Bronx Parents, Puerto Rican organizations, black organizations were coming up in the community. And we saw that they were giving out free food. And we saw that they were giving out clothes for the people, the needy. I said, to myself, *Why don't we do the same thing?*

For me, it wasn't about colors anymore. You see what I'm saying? It's not about flying colors anymore! And it wasn't about black or brown. We were one community. Stuck in the same disaster. Dealing with the same poverty. Same problems. The city, the government, they didn't care about any of us. The burning buildings, the drugs, the violence. They didn't care about ANY of us. It wasn't just the gangs. We were all in one community going through the same stuff. And the city looked at all of us, treated all of us, not just the gangs, ALL of us blacks and Puerto Ricans as savages. To the city, we were sub-humans that didn't deserve to live with proper services or a chance at a decent life.

So I wanted to change the condition of the community. I wanted to be a part of the solution. I didn't want to be a part of the problem; I couldn't be part of the problem anymore. So I started to change. We were still a gang, but the transition was about to happen; I was talking to the guys in a new way. And I remember the day my father found out that I was in a gang.

Some people in the community were saying, "Your son is here doing this and this. He's in that club over there." And my father comes in the Ghetto Brothers clubhouse. OH, MAN. And I'm talking to the guys, "Remember guys, by any means necessary. We gotta do this for the community." We had pictures of Campos and Malcolm X up on the wall. Very revolutionary. One of the guys comes up to me, "Yo, Benjy, this old man's looking for you."

I look, I said, "Oh, man, it's my pops!" So I'm walking this way, remember Soul Train? I'm walking through the middle of the guys like they were a Soul Train line. I'm looking down out of respect. He said, "Look up." I said, "Pa, I can explain —" "What are you doing here?" he asked, cutting me off. "I never taught you anything like this." He saw my jacket, he saw my hair. Remember, before I'd go home, I'd wash myself in the pump, comb my hair, take off the jacket. He caught me with everything on! So he takes me by the ear, in front of all the Ghetto Brothers, and he's walking me in the summer time, all the way from 163rd Street, all the way to 940 Tiffany Street. We lived on the top floor. He said, "Go upstairs." He was an old man, strong. "Go upstairs. Take a bath. I'm gonna deal with you." You know what I'm thinking? That's it, he's gonna do me in. I was his oldest son.

Even though he was older now, he was still a very strong man. I took a bath, came out. He said, "Sit down. Tell me the story. How did this happen?" I told him the WHOLE story. "Pa, in the end, give me a chance. I want to do something good for the community." He said, "I'm glad you told me the truth because I already knew everything about you. Everybody in the community told me. But you denied it to me. You held it back from me." I said, "Pa, I'm ashamed. I'm so sorry." He said, "All right. So, I'm gonna give you lock down." He locked me down; I couldn't go outside. Ghetto Brothers, that same week, they came around, "Yo, Benjy, man, we haven't seen you!" My brothers Victor and Robert were like, "He's home. My father's got him locked up." So they came on Tiffany, it was a sea of Ghetto Brothers, "YO, BENJY, COME

DOWNSTAIRS." I'm at the window, I look behind me and my father's standing right there. "I can't come outside, my dad doesn't want me to go out." They were all laughing, "Ahhhh…" I said, "I'll see you next week, guys." My father let me go out the next week. 'Cause he believed. I told him, "Papi, the things that you taught me, I'm teaching the Ghetto Brothers."

And it was true. I was trying to teach the Ghetto Brothers what my father had always taught me. What I had always known was right. But I knew that I needed help. I needed guidance. So I went to United Bronx Parents for help, to let them know that I, the Ghetto Brothers, wanted to work with them, help the community like they were helping the community. And soon, I went on T.V. with Miss Antonetty, the director of United Bronx Parents.

Ghetto Brothers headquarters was on 162nd Street; her organization was around the corner. United Bronx Parents Daycare Center was started in '67 or '66. But it was later in 1971, that was the first time that me and this lady had ever met; when we were on channel 13 together. She liked when I was talking revolutionary words, talking about change. She sees a young man, who's flying colors, but wasn't thinking like a gang, was thinking about bringing the community together.

Two weeks later, we went on television together. So she saw me that day, she saw me doing all this gesturing and she kept on looking at me. The following day, she comes into my club. "Benjy, there's this lady here." All the Ghetto Brothers turned around like this, "Can we help you?!" "Yeah, I'd like to talk to Benjy." "All right guys, get out the way... Oh, Miss Antonetty. Yeah, we were together." She said, "Would you like a job?" I said, "Sure." She said, "Go home and take a bath."

Remember, we were in that transition from gang to organization. We still had colors. And the Ghetto Brothers all went, "Ooo..." So I said, "I'll do that." So I went home, I took a bath. The following day, I went to United Bronx Parents. She offered me a job downstairs. And I noticed that in her organization there was a refrigerator for the truck to give out food for the kids in the program. I said, "Miss Antonetty, you think there's a possible way you could bring a truck like this to the Ghetto Brothers headquarters so we can give out free food to the kids in our community?" She said, "Yes!"

This lady knew a lot of revolutionary people at that time. There was a Puerto Rican nationalist group from the 1950s, went to the House of Congress, put themselves on the banister with handcuffs. And they were shooting at the Congress. That was back in the days. They arrested those people. And that lady, the leader of the group, was there. I walk into United Bronx Parents and Miss Antonetty said, "Benjy, look who's here." And I went, "Ohhh, Lolita Lebron." And I shook her hand and she said, "I read about you in jail." She told me that she read about me in jail. I couldn't believe that.

Lolita Lebron. Very famous revolutionary young lady who wanted Puerto Rican independence. So, I met her, and she looked like a Pentecostal lady, from the churches. Later on she was telling me that — I don't know if it's her son or daughter — the government said something, did something and her daughter was killed in a car accident in Puerto Rico. You know that it was a setup. I looked at her, man, you know, like you're staring. And I'm thinking to myself: *I'm looking at history!*

I have to say that Miss Antonetty was a beautiful person, somebody who really cared. She understood that I wanted to change and she believed in me. She was a tremendous help. She gave us the truck to give out free food. So the Ghetto Brothers started giving out free food to the people in our community. We needed clothes, she provided the clothes that the Ghetto Brothers started giving out. Miss Antonetty had a connection with all these people. So we started giving out food, clothing, and then we needed to clean the community. She provided the brooms. Joey Conzo, who has taken a lot of pictures of gang guys and stuff, he did not know this, and Miss Antonetty, that's his grandmother. He never knew any of this about his grandmother. And I knew Joey when he was a little boy and I was in the Ghetto Brothers around the corner. He said, "Benjy, my grandmother helped out the GBs?!" I told him, "Yes! We were a strong organization with your grandmother's help." I said, "It was them, United Bronx Parents, that provided the food, the clothing, the brooms, and also the political education."

Perry Thomas, the author of *Down These Mean Streets*, she invited him. She invited all of these revolutionary people. Perry Thomas wrote the book, *Down These Mean Streets*. Puerto Rican guy. A book about the streets of Harlem — Spanish Harlem — and the changes that went around in the Puerto Rican community during those years when the Puerto Ricans first came here: the discrimination, the hatred, the anger, the killings.

Miss Antonetty introduced me to some other people. Helena Valentine, another revolutionary individual. Oh, man, I met so many people. Also, when that was happening, I started to tell the Ghetto Brothers that we were going to shed our colors. By the time that the Black Panthers were all over the place, people started joining the Ghetto Brothers left and right. Why? Because now they didn't see a gang. They saw guys that wanted to help the community, that wanted to contribute something to the community. So they started to come in. Older guys. They'd come in and be like, "How old are you?" At that time I was 19. And these guys were like older guys. But they liked the platform of the Ghetto Brothers.

Plus, I had already gone through my revolutionary socialist and early political phase. And early on it was my boy Joseph Mpa who had the most political influence on me. Joseph Mpa. That was my boy. We've been together since day one. So it was him. He was working in affiliation with the Black Panthers on Boston Road. He said to me, "Benjy, why don't you direct all this energy. Instead of hurting one another, why don't we work to bring unity among our people. We gotta get our people together." And I was already thinking that, you know. Then after that, I was introduced to the young lords. Then after the Young Lords, I was introduced to the Puerto Rican Socialist Party. I stood with them, they were very well organized.

What I liked about the Puerto Rican Socialist Party was that they were intellectuals, university people, they knew organizations, they knew about how to put community organizations together. These guys were really intellectuals. In fact, I still got the book at home,

Introduction to Socialism, they gave that book to me. But I left the organization.

One day, they had a big meeting. They were discussing the Palestinians and Israel conflict. And I went, "Wait, wait, wait, what is this?" I said, "No, I ain't buying that." They said, "Why?" And I told them who I was, that I was Jewish. They said, "Are you serious?" "That's right!" From then on, I left the organization. I said, "I don't want to be with you guys." 'Cause they were like, "Death to Israel… Kill the Jews…" No. I wasn't with that. So I left them alone from then on.

•••

As far as social programs that we created, the first thing we did was we started to give out food. United Bronx Parents provided us with a refrigerator truck, and in the morning we used to give out food to the children. We drove it right over where the Ghetto Brothers club was. On 162nd Street, right around the corner on Westchester was United Bronx Parents. 162nd between Prospect and 163rd Street. Right around the corner from the Ghetto Brothers club, there was Westchester Avenue, where the train was. Well, United Bronx Parents was there.

After the food drive, we started the free clothes drive. What people would do is donate clothes, I mean some really good clothes. And we would give it to some kids or people that were poor, which was basically the whole community, you know, people that couldn't afford it. We'd give the clothes to them.

And then the final drive that we did was a cleaning drive. We cleaned and swept the community. United

Bronx Parents, again, gave us the brooms. That was really nice of Miss Antonetty. I loved and respected that woman so much, Dr. Evelina Antonetty. She gave us the brooms, so we were sweeping up the block. So people would see that, you know, *Look, look at these young guys and look what they're doing. They're cleaning up the community. Their cleaning up the streets!* We were taking care of the garbage over here because the landlords weren't doing their work and the supers were lazy, and a lot of these supers were not around. So we took care of everything.

And this was a huge problem, the absence of the supers. It was terrible, a lot of these supers were never around. In those days, you had guys taking drugs on the roof and stuff. A lot of these supers came around, maybe one hour, just came around looking at the place and walked away. So they tried to give the impression to the people that they were doing something, but everybody knew that they weren't doing nothing at all. So what did the Ghetto Brothers do? We went up there, we swept the buildings, we mopped the buildings, we took care of business, and you know, we left a good example. We didn't walk up to the super and say, "Yo, man, you guys…" Look, he doesn't wanna do the job, we'll take care of it 'cause we're here. I had a lot of guys anyway.

Another thing that we did was start an educational program. When the Ghetto Brothers started the educational program, we encouraged the brothers who knew how to read to teach the Ghetto Brothers who didn't know how to read. So we had people coming in, we had the pamphlets for the Puerto Rican Socialist Party. And we had the Black Panthers. Not so much the Young

Lords. These people from the orgainzation were coming in, giving us educational paraphernalia so the guys could read, see films, and encourage them to be well informed. And, of course, United Bronx Parents was also giving us information.

We were very busy doing a lot of things in our community. What we were tempted to do was walk up to the landlords and say, "Listen, we mopped, we swept, we took out your garbage, man. You should give us some money." But we didn't do that. And besides, these guys hardly ever came around.

Another big problem in those days was the social services. The sad thing about it, back in those days, the social services were terrible. Like look at Lincoln hospital. The Young Lords had to take over their X-Ray truck to provide that service to the people in the community. They took over an X-Ray truck. There was some Savage Nomads involved in that also.

And you had doctors that lived way out of the city, you know. They'd come into the city to do their job or get by. Most people in the community didn't have any money. Some people didn't have insurance. Some people were not on welfare at the time; and welfare was a big thing back in those days. So you had people that were being turned out from the doctors, *Oh, listen, you have no insurance, you have no money, well, I'm sorry, we can't take care of you. Unless it's a really, really, really bad emergency where we can bring you to the ER.* They'd patch the guy up, then after that we see the same guy walking down the street — when he should be staying in the hospital. The city government didn't care about this. They wanted it to be like this. They wanted everybody in the South Bronx to just drop dead, just like the article, like President Ford said, they wanted all of us in the South Bronx to just drop dead!

And you have, for instance, YSA, Youth Services Agency. They wanted to hire gang Presidents, get them a job, call them paraprofessionals, to keep them off the street. 'Cause you figure, if you can get these brothers — the leaders of these gangs — and give them jobs, keep them off the street, their members will not be getting into trouble. This is their way of quailing down the violence.

Then I said, "But wait!" We started to realize that there was only a portion of that money given to us, maybe $65, $100. Then, we found out later on that there was supposed to be way more money allocated to the people in this community, for the service in the community. And the people in charge of administering, distributing this money, they were taking this money and pocketing it for themselves. Found out later on that the guy who handled the YSA, this guy was taking a lot of money. And he was found him dead in his car. He was murdered, nobody knew who did it. But we knew. "Yo, Benjy, yo, Charlie? What happened? We were suppose to get more money?" "What happened?" Yo, these people they were pocketing this money. And it came from the federal government to the state and then to these organizations that were supposed to provide the money to us, supposed to help us. What happened? Well, we only got a portion of it. These guys pocketed the rest of the money.

Another really sad thing is that in those days, EVERYBODY was on welfare. I mean practically EVERYBODY! There were no jobs! There used to be jobs and proper services. The Bronx used to be beautiful. It was bustling with businesses and stores, and people had jobs. But then when the buildings started coming down and the city just neglected the Bronx, man... And the Cross Bronx Expressway had already ripped a hole through the middle of the Bronx. That thing, what Moses did, had already set problems in motion. "Model city?" Big laugh! What "Model City?" Model city tried to establish something, they failed! You got some organizations that tried to help the community, they did their best. But a lot of times, we felt that a lot of these leaders were about greed. So instead of helping the community, they were taking this money in. So the people in the Bronx were getting hit from every angle: the city and the very people who were supposed to be trying to help the situation.

And that's why so many people were enrolling in welfare. They had nothing else. They had no choice. Their livelihood had been taken away. And this wasn't no accident. People like Robert Moses didn't care what happened to black and brown people in the South Bronx. And anyway, welfare wasn't much. How could a family expect to live off of what you got from welfare? When I went to the Welfare Department on Morris, there were tons of people there. I mean, people were complaining: They needed money, they needed food, they needed to pay the rent. And you know, the guys who were taking care of the people, the people in charge at welfare, a lot of these people were stressed out because they had a lot of case loads — MANY people. It was like the whole South Bronx was on welfare during this time.

So I'm seeing all of this, I'm realizing that it's not even about colors anymore, because the gangs were contributing to making a bad situation even worse. I was realizing this, owning up to the part, the role that I had played in all of this — being a savage, running wild and doing hurtful stuff that other gang members were doing. Then Ford came to the Bronx. President Ford comes to the Bronx and is like, *Drop dead.* The city badly needed money at that time, you know, the New York City fiscal crises and all that stuff, and he told the city, "Drop Dead," that was the headline in the paper. The city needed money. Where the hell was all the money? The Government is suppose to be bringing this money to the state, all the way down to the city. And then you read the papers and this guy over here gets caught taking money; this guy over there stealing money over here. And we're saying to each other, *See, the money that was suppose to be brought here to help the Bronx, to help bring up jobs, employment — these guys are taking the money for their own purposes.* And remember, the landlords were making money from burning their own buildings. Everybody knew what was going on.

See, when President Ford came to the South Bronx, he not only went to the Bronx, he came to the other boroughs, too. But the South Bronx was the worst place out of all of the boroughs. The South Bronx was a deathtrap. The ugliest place on the earth was the South Bronx. It was torn apart, broken, and just gutted out. The conditions were terrible. So President Ford came to the South Bronx. He made a lot of promises. Many promises were made. *Aw, we're gonna do this. We're gonna build these buildings. Aw, we're gonna...* He never did it. He didn't do it! So a lot of people were just talking. These guys, "Oh, we're gonna do whatever we can to rebuild the city, to bring employment." Only to go back to Washington to say, "Drop dead!" to New York.

It was all politics. It was all politics. *Oh, if the Hispanic community see that Ford went over there, aw, man, let's vote for this man! Let's vote for him who came to see us. And he made promises to us, so guess what? Let's repay the man, let's vote for him again.* It's all politics.

Politicians always came around during the time before the elections, they would always come promising food, promising clothing, promising better health care, promising better housing. But what was the keyword? VOTE! *You want all of this? Yeah. Vote for me, and I'll be there for you.* Only when you vote for them, you'll never get anything.

But there were some people trying to get things done despite all of this. You had United Bronx Parents — Dr. Evelina Antonetty. Then you had another lady, Olga Mendez. You had the Black Panthers. Then you had the Young Lords. Then you had other organizations. And you had the American Legion, ex-veterans from WWII, the Korean War. All these organizations did their best to try to make the situation in the Bronx a little better. And these people, from United Bronx Parents to Olga, had organizations where they invited people to come in to eat. Where they invited people to come hear lectures.

In other words, they did all of this to keep hope alive. To demonstrate that there is hope out there. To say, "See, we don't need to depend on these people. We can do this ourselves. Let's get together. Let's put our resources together. Let's stop the violence. Let's stop the fighting. We can do something, but we have to work together." Miss Antonetty did everything she could to try to get jobs to young people, which she did. She did a hell-of-a-job of bringing money from the state to help hire young people for the summer. And this was the time when things were bad, I mean really terrible. But there were kids working. She even found ways to have them working within the organization. She'd say, "Listen, I'll pay you so and so if you can clean these streets for me." But at least she did it. And all of this was showing me that it was not about colors anymore.

Remember, when I first moved to the South Bronx, it was nice. It was a very nice place. I mean, there were bakery shops, there were pharmacies, there were stores, you know, bodegas, there were laundromats. The streets were clean. People had jobs. It was nice. I remember at that time we used to go to Woolworth's. A lot of people had money then and they used to go to Woolworth's to buy their little variety of things and their clothes and a little jewelry here and there. There was a bank across the street, the bank of Spain, very prosperous at the time. Chase Manhattan bank was there. The place was nice! You had four movie theaters, four active theaters on Prospect Avenue — Loewes, the Berlin Theater, the RKO, and the Persian around the corner. I mean, that place was buzzing with businesses. There wasn't any drugs; there weren't any junkies; there weren't a lot of prostitutes roaming around the streets; you didn't have anything to fear in the streets. You walked out of your house, you didn't have to worry about somebody stabbing you, somebody killing you.

But then, when the fires started to come in, when the Bronx started burning and the buildings started coming down, many of these businesses and the people just packed up and moved out. And those that could afford it went to Co-Op City in the North Bronx. The typical South Bronx family couldn't afford to live up there, though. We saw pictures of these beautiful buildings, we said, "This is fantastic." But you know, ay, we can't live around there. We don't look like those people. We can't even walk around that community, especially Arthur Avenue, the Italian community. If any brother, or anybody not like them walked in that community, forget it, I mean, you're dead!

Here's the Italian community in the midst of the South Bronx. Very prosperous community. But they had a habit of looking at us differently. One time, this guy said to me, "Yo, get outta here. We don't want you around here." So I told him, "What's the trouble?" But when the gang situation started to rise up and I approached some Italians, it was different, "Ay, you're surrounded, man," I said to this one Italian guy. "I mean, you're in this little enclave over here. So you're in no position to be telling people to get outta here. 'Cause where you gonna go? You're gonna have to get your cars to get out of here. You have to pass by our block. You have to go to the train station. So you're gonna have to go up around my block. How would you feel if I said, 'You ain't going nowhere?'"

But while the Italian community was shielded, treated nicely and stayed prosperous, our community in the South Bronx was a disaster. It was really terrible back in those days. Man, even sleeping was difficult — *If* you slept! I remember looking out the window, I would sleep next to the bed and I would look out my window to make sure that nobody's, you know, coming into my building. I had to watch out for my family. I had to be on guard. You know, looking across the street, looking at the moon. Looking at brothers walking up and down. Looking at junkies on the corner, just to make sure that nothing would happen. So if I heard any sound, man, I was just gonna get up. 'Cause I'm thinking of my father, my brothers, my sister, my mother. And thank God nothing happened to us. But I always had that open eye — always.

But having to live like this affected my sleep big time! Because I don't know who's going to come through my building. I don't know who's going to come through the fire escape. I don't know if somebody's gonna steal the pipes down here; which they did when I lived on Park Street. We were in this nice building. Only as years went by, it started to break down. People went into the basement, stole the pipes. Then we didn't have water. I said to my father, "There's no water!" My father said, "Yeah, because they're stealing it."

So like I said, that's when he took my family, moved us out, moved us around the corner on Tiffany Street. Rememer, my father saw this building, and it was still kind of nice, but it was boarded up in the front with a chain. He broke the door down. And he found an apartment right there. And he said, "The miracle was that there was still hot water."

So we lived there. Nobody lived in that building. We lived there for a little while, for one month. Then he took my family to 940 Tiffany Street, on the last floor. That was one of the best apartments we ever had. But my father was constantly looking out for his family. He said, "Where's my family gonna live? Well, we're going to go to look at this place." We found it across the street.

But we were fortunate. We were fortunate to have my father. Fortunate that he did what he did. But most people were not that fortunate, you know. The chaos was still all around. I remember, I never forgot this, that on Prospect Avenue, there was a guy on the ground, he was unarmed, and a cop shot him right there. I never forgot that. It was a junkie. The cop had him on the ground and the guy was just trying to move away, and BOOM!!!! The cop shot him! I was like, "YO, what the hell is going on?" I was young, so look at the impression that was sowed into my mind — our minds back in those days. Our lives were cheap to the cops. The cop just shot him. The guy had no weapon.

And here's the thing. I used to walk up to police officers and ask them, "How come you people don't talk to us? How come every time you look at us, you wanna hit us, you wanna beat us, or you wanna shoot us? Well, how would you feel if we did the same thing to you? I mean, talk to us, man. Do you always have to hit? Do you have to always harass us? Do you always have to push us? Do you always have to pull our hair? Do you always have to threaten us because you got your guns there? Don't pick on innocent people out here in the street. Stop it, already." And the cops would just laugh.

So things like this, my eyes were opening. What do you call it? It was an awakening. I was having an awakening. For me, it wasn't about flying colors anymore. I wanted to take responsibility for our actions. I felt that the gangs were contributing to the problem in the South Bronx and we needed to stop. I believed that the Ghetto Brothers could be an organization for real change.

Of course, not everybody agreed with this. Some GBs didn't want to change. So in 1971, when we started the transition from the gang to an organization, we were still a gang. Everybody still knew us as a gang. But the change was coming. I had a new vision for the Ghetto Brothers. And this feeling that I was having, it was making me feel good about myself for the first time in a long while.

Chapter 9
Power Fuerza

1971 was a pivotal year. We were trying to transition from a gang to an organization, which wasn't easy because some GBs wasn't down with that. Plus, the reality was, the other gangs were still growing. Things were still what they were; the gang era was happening. So the transition was slow at first. There were realities of gang life that had to be dealt with. No matter what, you always had to be on guard, you know. But even still, we had fun, we partied, and, of course, we played music!

That summer, we, the Ghetto Brothers band, recorded our one and only album, *Power Fuerza*. In 1969, we had officially changed the name of our band from Los Junior Beatles to the Ghetto Brothers. We were already growing, getting older. The Junior Beatles didn't fit us anymore. I still liked Beatles songs at the time, but that wasn't who we were anymore. So we changed the name.

When we recorded *Power Fuerza*, the members in the band were Franky — Franky Valentin, my brother Robert, my brother Victor, me, and David Silva, who was my cousin. He wasn't my blood cousin. We called him our cousin 'cause he was raised with us. David is an honorary Melendez, 'cause he fit our songs and he played fantastic. And there was Chiqui Concepción. He's the cousin of Bernie Williams, the former Yankees baseball player. Chiqui once said to me, "Benjy, man, if you can get me one of the Ghetto Brothers albums, I'll get you one of

Bernie Williams' bats." Oh, man, Chiqui really wanted a copy of *Power Fuerza*. That's because our *Power Fuerza* album is rare. It's a collector's item for people who are into vinyl and rare records. It's known among DJs all over the world. Big hit with funk, Latin funk, and soul DJs. Also in the band, there was Angelo Garcia and Luis "Bull" Bristo. Luis Bristo was the drummer.

Each band member contributed something. Chiqui Conceptión — Ghetto Brother gang member. A very good congo player; he played percussion. Him and Franky; both of them were fantastic. Chiqui Conceptión was very quiet. Franky was a Ghetto Brother; he was in the gang. Then you have my brother Robert. Cool guy, but don't cross him! He's got that natural strength about him. So when him and my brother Victor were in cahoots, if anything happened, they both had each other's back. You do something to him, you're gonna have to do something to the other guy. So I had to try to quail these guys down.

Luis Bristo, "Bull," he was in the Ghetto Brothers gang, of course, a known member. This guy was powerful! This guy was a bull! One day, we were in the club, Ghetto Brother's clubhouse, he comes in and he yells, "Fernando?" Fernando, another GB, was talking to another Ghetto Brother, and Bull took him and beat the daylights out of him because he got fresh with his girl. I'd never seen that guy like that before. That's why we called him Bull. He just rushed him, picked him up, slammed him — BOOM!!!! The only members in the Ghetto Brothers band that were not in the Ghetto Brothers gang was my brother Robert and my cousin David Silva. Like I said, Robert was too young at the time, but he was still around.

When we did the *Power Fuerza* album, our style of music was different from when we began when we were Los Junior Beatles. Originally, I wanted to keep The Beatles style of music. And a lot of our original songs were, to me, very Beatles like. It was my brother Victor who changed the whole concept of the band. Victor was really smart about music, and he was very wide in his musical taste. He liked Sly and The Family Stone and James Brown. He loved soul and funk and rock. He used to say, "If you got people tapping their feet, if you got them doing that, then they like the music." One day, he said to me, "Why don't we mix it up? Benjy, I know that you like The Beatles, but let's start expanding. Let's mix it up. Let's play some Santana type of music, some soul over here, and Beatles and put it all together. And you're gonna get a blend of a lot of things."

It was Victor who changed our musical direction. And he was the choreographer of the band, the conductor and arranger, you know. Victor was the one who guided everything in the Ghetto Brothers band. I was the lead singer, but Victor ran the show in the band. He was the leader of the Ghetto Brothers band. That's why we used to call him the choreographer of the band. He was the one that guided everything.

Victor was fantastic! He had a great ear. One time, he looked at my brother Robert and he said, "Your E is out." Robert looked down at his guitar and sure enough, it was. Victor used to call me Ray Charles. He used to call me that because every song we did, I had a habit of saying, "Ooh, my baby." So he goes, "Yo, yo, Ray Charles. Stop that, man! You gotta change that tune." So he was the one who said, "All right, Benjy, do this voice and let Robert do this over here." But I mean, Victor was fantastic. He could have done the whole album by himself if he wanted to. 'Cause he played lead guitar, rhythm guitar, bass, drums, trombone, piano. Victor played everything! The guy was tremendously talented.

I remember there was this one time at the 3rd Street Music School. The city was paying money for the Ghetto Brothers — since we had a musical band — to join. That's who got us into East 3rd Street Music School, it was the city. It's right there on the East Side, East 3rd Street, where the Hell's Angels were, right there on the same block. One of the best music schools in New York. So they wanted us to go there to learn how to read music. So when we got there, the guy looked at us and said, "Let me see what you can do." So we started to play. And he turned to Dominguez, who had brought us there, and goes, "Where the hell did you get these guys?" Then to us he says, "Who taught you these things?" "Everything we do is by ear," I said. So channel 7 comes into the place one day. They told the guy who ran the place, I forgot his name, "Give us your best band here." He goes, "They're right there," and he pointed to us. So we did some songs and they recorded it. This was, man, '73, after *Power Fuerza*. And you get what I'm saying? Out of all of the bands that he had in that place, he said, "This is my best band here!"

The way we got connected to the school was through the city, under our manager Manny Dominguez. They got in contact with Manny. And they said, "Listen, we'd like to pay for these guys to learn how to play music." And I found it difficult. I said, "I really need to hear that. I can do it this way." He said, "You know, Benjamin, that's pretty good." My brother Victor was the one who taught us all of this. Dominguez was the one who bought instruments for us. He was a school teacher. He invested money in the band. This was before *Power Fuerza*. He saw the potential. He said, "You know what? I'm gonna buy you guys instruments." So he bought everybody in the band an instrument. That was the best.

So when the opportunity came to do the album, we were ready, man. And at this point, despite all of the gang stuff, I was hopeful. I was thinking about how we, the people, could get power. So that's how the album title came about. "Fuerza" in Spanish means power. So the name of the album translated to "Power, Power." Power, two times! You had the English power and the Spanish power combined.

And you know, it was funny how the album came about and how we first met Bobby Marin. The people in the community, there was some guys, men, went to Salsa Records — Mary Lou's — on Prospect Avenue. "Hey, Mary Lou? Listen, you gotta go over there, you gotta check these guys out, man. Every Friday, they play in the street and gather a large crowd." So Mary Lou — his real name is Ishmael something, I can't pronounce his last name; it's on the album cover credits — comes over and checks us out. Then he said, "How would you guys like to record an album?" We were young, so you can imagine our reaction. We were like, *Aw, man*!

But before that, there was a burglary. They thought that we, the Ghetto Brothers gang, stole some instruments from them. 'Cause we were the only club in the area, the closest ones to the store. A couple days after the burglary, Bobby Marin, the producer, came to the clubhouse. He thought we had did it. And then a couple days later, I went over there to Mary Lou's. I went over there to clear my name. I said, "Listen, Mary Lou, we don't do things like that around here." Later on, he apologized to us. He liked what me and Robert did and he told us to pick any guitar we wanted.

So the day we actually recorded the album, everything was cool. We did the whole album in one day. All of the songs were recorded in one day. We started recording in the afternoon and finished before evening. It was at Finetone Studio. We just went in there, and just recorded.

The songs that we did were: "Ghetto Brother Power," which is our signature song; "You Say That You're My Friend;" "There is Something in My Heart;" "Viva Puerto Rico Libre;" "I Saw a Tear," and "Mastica Chupa Y Jala," which for the first time I found out what that meant. Victor wrote that song. He did the whole thing, the arrangement. I said, "Robert, what does that mean?" In Spanish "Mastica" means to chew, "chupa" means to suck, and "Jala" means to pull. I said, "What is that?" "That's smoke," he said. "What?!" "That's what Victor was talking about." I did not know that. I thought it was about sex. He said, "No, no, no, it was about smoke. Victor was talking about smoking weed in that song."

And we had the song "Girl From the Mountain." That song was about a Puerto Rican girl. There was this guy named Felix Tollinchi; that was his song, he wrote that. He was of the Harvey Averne Barrio Band. It was about a girl that he loved that lived in PR. Felix wasn't an official

Ghetto Brother, he was a friend who used to hang around with us and he played with us, but he was never a Ghetto Brother. He did that song, "Girl From the Mountain," on another album. But he liked the way that we did it, so he gave it to us.

We also did this song called "Got This Happy Feeling." That song was a mistake, that's a blooper. We thought we had finished recording. Then, Mary Lou says, "Guys, you got one more song." I said, "Man, I don't have no more songs." So Victor said, "Benjy, you know that tune that you did, "Got This Happy Feeling?'" "Yeah." "Why don't you do that, why don't you just say anything? Just play with your voice." If you listen to the record, I don't sing fluently like that, I'm playing around. And you know what they did, the engineers? They recorded it. And when the album came out, I said, "What? Are you serious? What is this?!" And the guys were laughing, "Benjy, leave it, man, as a joke. Just leave it."

Victor had known about the song already. I told him about it and sang some of it for him. And he remembered. The song was about MayLin. But I didn't finish writing the words. She was having my baby. And I was happy. I was excited that she was having my child, my first child! I was so elated. Oh, my goodness. Me and Victor wrote all of the songs on the album. It's even. The only song that's not ours is "Girl From the Mountain." "Ghetto Brother Power," that was written by Victor. Yeah, that was Victor. That was Victor's tune!

I'm very proud of the album we did. *Power Fuerza* could've have been bigger back then. But we didn't know anything about the music business. We were paid 500 bucks to do the whole album. We were street kids, what did we know. Just $500, that's it. And we were like, "Oh...Wow!" Like we struck it rich. And we didn't know anything about contracts. Victor and Robert were under age, so they forged my parents name. We had no idea about rights or any of that stuff. We were just happy to be in a real studio recording an album.

And even still, I was focused on the Ghetto Brothers club. We were transitioning from a gang to an organization. Everything was right there and then. Before we did *Power Fuerza*, the music was always there for the purpose of calming your nerves, making you happy, relaxing the Ghetto Brothers, in a good mood, a party mood. So the music was, what's the saying? "Soothing to the savage beast." So that's what we did. And I knew that there was a time to practice and a time to deal with the gang/organization. So, most of the time, after we finished having meetings with other gangs here and there, when we came back, to get our frustrations off, we'd play music. But it was a lot being in a band and being in the GBs. It was hard for me to focus on both.

With the band, even though I was the lead singer, I was more in and out, in and out. Robert and Victor spent a lot more time with the band, practicing and rehearsing. Maybe if I'd spent more time with the band, the Ghetto Brothers band could have been something big. We had a great sound. The people in the community loved us. And the album was great. But I don't have any regrets. I wanted to deal with the Ghetto Brothers organization. I was trying to make a change. 'Cause I was concerned about the community. I was concerned about what was happening in the community more than I was about pursuing a recording career. Maybe I should've tried to do both. Maybe I missed out on a great opportunity, you know, for the Ghetto Brothers band to be something big. I mean, we were young, but we were really good. But at that time, I believed that what I was trying to do for the community was more important. So that's what I focused on, trying to save lives.

Because it was terrible, man. The Bronx was just awful! And there really wasn't too many people trying to fix it, especially among the gangs. But at the same time, my brother re-cultured me. He helped me with the music. And the music helped keep me sane. Plus, Victor's teachings made me understand music much better. He said to me, "All right, Benjy. You're going to play this and you're going to sing this song." Victor was the one who did it all. Victor was the one who pulled all the strings, it was Victor. He taught me so much. But my head was more focused on the Ghetto Brothers and the community. That's what I was in the middle of. I was in the middle of the street gang wars, all the poverty, and despair. I wanted to try to find a way out for the community. That's what I wanted to work for. The Ghetto Brothers band came second.

After we did *Power Fuerza*, we never pursued trying to do another album. For one thing, Mary Lou didn't ask us to. But we just went on doing our own little thing. *Aw, man, you know what. Let's just play. Let's go to the roof and play. Let's go in the basement and play.* That was my attitude. But we didn't really pursue it. We had our fantasies, though. Being on television. We saw ourselves on the "Ed Sullivan Show." We saw ourselves looking like that. Being on television, playing our music, having our fans going crazy. That was the fantasy that we all wanted to live. As years went by, we were all over television in a different way. So in some small way, it materialized. But do I feel like the Ghetto Brothers band missed a big opportunity? Yes, I believe we missed a huge opportunity. But what are you gonna do? I have no regrets, I believe I made the right decision.

Still, *Power Fuerza* is a classic. In fact, it's being reissued. So I have no regrets about what could've happened with the band. My mind was on the community, ending the gang violence, changing things for the better. I guess the Ghetto Brothers band was one of my sacrifices.

Chapter 10
Black Benjie and the Peace Meeting

We recorded *Power Fuerza* in the summer of 1971. I was feeling good. Despite all the gang stuff, I was on a real high, very excited. That fall/winter, December, is when everything happened with my brother Black Benjie.

I met Black Benjie around the summer of 1971. Charlie introduced Black Benjie to me. I called him Black Benjie 'cause he was Benjamin, Cornell. His last name was Benjamin, first name Cornell. And I told him, "The reason I call you that is because I'm Yellow Benjy, so you're gonna be Black Benjie." Charlie introduced me to him. This guy was a gentleman, he was charming. Black Benjie and I were getting closer as friends.

But before going further about Black Benjie, let me tell you how I met Charlie, Charlie Suarez, who introduced me to Black Benjie. I was on 158th Street. And I saw this guy practicing, "HI-YAH!!!!" And he breaks this piece of wood in half. I was with Raymond. The laundry was next door. That's where my girlfriend MayLin, who later became my wife, used to live, the Chinese laundry. I saw this guy, and I'm looking at him. And I said to Raymond, "Did you see what that guy did? He broke that wood in half!" Remember, we were into martial arts. So I went up to this guy and I said, "Hello, my name is Benjy." He was like, "Yeah, O.K., and?" He looked at me with no concern, you know, like he thought I could be a threat and he was playing it cool. "No, no," I said. I didn't want to alarm him. I said, "I was impressed with what you did." This was before I was in a gang. We were not a gang yet, we were friends. It was later when we'd become the club, the gang. But that's how I *first* met Charlie.

Later on, after the Savage Nomads days, Charlie wasn't around then. Between the transition from the gang and the organization, that's when I looked at Charlie and I said, "Charlie, I'm gonna make you President." I did this for a reason. Charlie was heavy into dope. I didn't know anything about drugs at that time. Like I said, if you nodded off in front of me, as far as I'm concerned, you were tired. This is how ignorant I was to drugs at that time. So, I didn't know. Only way I knew anything about drugs was when my brother Victor told me about everything. So when I found out about Charlie using dope — because I loved Charlie so much, you know, he was like a brother to me — I made him President. I figured that he'd be too busy to do dope because there's a lot of Ghetto Brothers he would have to deal with. He would have to deal with a lot of these brothers who'd keep him so busy that he wouldn't have time to do dope. That's what I thought.

Then Charlie actually started believing that he was the *Supreme* President of the Ghetto Brothers, after all this gang stuff, and he left. He started telling people that he was the Supreme President. Charlie was telling people that he was the Supreme President, that he was over me!

Like I said, I only made Charlie President to help him stop doing dope. I didn't give him a position over me. I told all my friends, "If this guy really was the Supreme President, that means what? Whatever anybody else says, you gotta go by what Charlie says, right?" Well, guess what? After what happened with Black Benjie, you know what Charlie was doing? He was mobilizing the Ghetto Brothers for war. When I came to 158th Street where he was I said, "What are you doing, Charlie?" "Rah, rah…" Whatever he said. Then I said, "You know what? GBs, STAND DOWN! You ain't going nowhere!" Who did they listen to? They didn't listen to him. They listened to me! My youngest brother, Robert, who's been my witness, said, "Benjy, I just thought about something. Did you know that most of the Ghetto Brothers did not acknowledge Charlie as the Supreme President? You made him President of that Chapter, the first chapter, 'Cause all the Ghetto Brothers looked up to you and listened to you."

Now Rita Fecher, who did the film with Henry Chalfant, she's dead now, her husband, Dominguez, used to cater to Charlie. One day, we went to this loft downtown on Wooster Street. And Dominguez says to me, "I just realized something and I told Rita. I just realized that *this* is the guy pulling the strings, here." He was talking about me. He knew who was really the leader. Charlie didn't like the politics. I brought the politics. The liberation of the people. He didn't want none of that. He wasn't completely with helping the community, which was my focus and the direction that I was moving the Ghetto Brothers in. He tried to talk it, but that wasn't really him. After Black Benjie, he started to phase away. And I continued with the organization from there on in. I said, "You're not going to use my boys for your bidding. It doesn't work like that." So you know how many people call me? Ex-Ghetto Brothers, "Yo, Benjy! Look what this guy is doing. Yo, Benjy. Why is Charlie calling himself that?"

When I heard about this, I said, "'Supreme President?!' I never made him *Supreme* President."

O.K., so Black Benjie! Black Benjie was introduced to me by Charlie. This was 1971. October, 1971. Charlie says to me, "Benjy, this is my boy right here, Cornell Benjamin." I looked at him up and down. 25 years old. He worked as a drug counselor. I shook his hand. "So tell me about yourself?" I said. "I work over here…" Nice guy. He was older than me. Still, we got very close.

I saw the way that he was interacting with GBs and other people, you know. Remember, right there at this point, we were already transitioning from the Ghetto Brothers gang to the Ghetto Brothers organization. We had the Lee jackets, but we weren't really wearing colors too much, we had barets. I noticed the way he was talking to kids. He would go on one knee and talk to them, very friendly person. I wrote a song about that. I got a song about him. And he's looking at them. And every time the kids would run to Benjie, I said to myself, this guy's fantastic! Then I made an announcement to the Ghetto Brothers, I said, "You know what? Let's drop the Warlords, and let's start making Peace Ambassadors. I'm gonna make Benjie my 3rd Staff Leader." So he was the first Ghetto Brothers Peace Ambassador.

Black Benjie had come into the club and by a week later, he was staying in the Ghetto Brothers clubhouse. It was just a week later, he said, "Benjy, can I stay here?" I said, "Sure!" He didn't go home. So he calls me the next morning at my home, 940 Tiffany. "Benjy, can you bring me some breakfast? I'm hungry." "No problem." I brought him some food. We were close, I loved him like a brother.

And he was well-liked by everybody.

So that day, that sad day in December — it was a cold day. Black Benjie was murdered December 2, 1971. That day, I'd given him some food and everything as usual. That afternoon, Ghetto Brothers informants come in, "Benjy, three gangs are coming down, man. Seven Immortals, Black Spades, and the Mongols. They're coming to get the Roman Kings!" That was the gang right around the corner from us, remember? You can see the Roman Kings in the movie *Ain't Gon Eat My Mind*. Those young kids. Those are Roman Kings! When you see *Ain't Gonna Eat My Mind* and you see the kids running up and down these wooden things, those are them. When you see the little black brother and he looks at the camera, that's Bobby. He was the President. Like I said, those kids were BAD!!!! They were little, but they were BAD!!!! But we protected them 'cause they were a little club. So if gangs wanted to get at the Roman Kings, they had to go through Ghetto Brothers, and we were diplomats, "Yo, leave them alone, man."

So these three gangs were coming down, they were coming for the Roman Kings. I looked at the Ghetto Brothers, Charlie wasn't there at that moment, he came to the clubhouse right after they had left. So I said to Willlie, "Willie?" Willie Vasquez was one of the main Ghetto Brothers, the guy was a good warrior. And I looked at Black Benjie and I went, "Benjie? Your job is cut out for you, this is your day." He said, "Benjy, what do you want me to do?" He got up, no hesitation! I told him, "This job is cut out for you, Ben. Go get me the President, Vice President, and Warlords of those gangs. Bring them to the Ghetto Brothers clubhouse so we can broker a peace treaty with the Roman Kings and the three gangs. He said, "You got it, Ben." So he went to Horseshoe Park on Rogers and 165th Street. I thought he would be safe. I thought he had at least *twenty* Ghetto Brothers with him; I thought nothing was going to happened to him. Here I am thinking, all this time, that twenty Ghetto Brothers went with him.

I saw Willie a few summers ago, who was there when Black Benjie was killed. I said, "Willie, do you remember when I sent you?" "Yes, Benjy." "How many Ghetto Brothers did I send you with?" "There was only seven of us." "Wait, I'm thinking twenty." "No, Benjy. You sent Black Benjy, plus seven GBs. You said, 'No weapons.' So Black Benjie was walking ahead of us. We went down Rogers Street. We looked to the right and there was a sea of people. We went onto the edge of the stairs, Black Benjie walked ahead and he put up his hands and said, 'Peace, my brothers!' There was an Immortal on the other side with a pipe. Another Immortal had a machete. The guy with the pipe, said, 'Peace, SHIT!' Black Benjie said, 'Tip, tip!!!! Then, BOOM!!!! The brother with the pipe hits Black Benjie in the head. We split, it was only seven of us."

Black Benjie had told the other Ghetto Brothers to run. So GBs are running up the stairs. The guys turned around — the guys are telling me the story back at the clubhouse, and they saw those gangs just swarm on Black Benjie. The guys had turned around, Playboy had taken out his belt before he ran, but what are you gonna do with a belt against all those guys? They got Black Benjie in the corner at the bottom of the stairs. The guys said, "Benjy, all we saw was this dark sea of people just go right behind him. All you hear was screaming."

I'm sitting in the clubhouse. Charlie's sitting here, with his wife, Evelyn. A Ghetto Brother runs in, "Charlie, they're beating up Black Ben!" Charlie goes, "Nah, come on, that's not happening." I looked at Charlie. When Playboy ran in, a second Ghetto Brother, "Benjy, they're beating up Black Ben! Let's go!" I told the Ghetto Brothers, "LET'S GO!" So we ran to the ramp, went down the stairs saw all this blood. Lots of blood. Oh, my goodness. I said, "All right, you and you, go to Lincoln Hospital. And call us." We had a phone in the club. So they took Black Benjie to Lincoln Hospital. An hour later, we got a phone call. "Benjy, he's dead." I said, "What happened?" "His head was split four ways. He was stabbed multiple times, they broke everything in his body." And I just burst into tears. "No, that can't happen…" It was my fault. I was the one who sent him to make peace. I felt terrible.

In just over an hour's time, I never seen so many gang leaders in my life. There were gangs even coming from different boroughs to the Bronx. My block was getting filled with gang leaders. So I said, "I'm going to the 2nd division." Because my 2nd division was a warrior division. These guys were ready to roll. I go up there, Charlie was *already* there. Charlie was ready to mobilize the biggest gang war in Bronx history. This would've been chronicled as the greatest gang battle in the history of New York City. And guess what? Fort Apache would have earned its name that day.

Things could've have gone really crazy. Remember, at the time I had made Charlie President. I wanted to give him some responsibility, something to help him stop using dope. That's how much I loved this guy; he was like a brother to me. So I made him President. But my brother, Robert, told me, "Benjy, I want you to understand something. When you made Charlie President, did you know that no Ghetto Brother knew about the deal? The only people that knew he was President is our division. Because no Ghetto Brother recognized him, they recognized you." So Charlie was never recognized as the Supreme President, he was only the President of the first Ghetto Brothers division. So when Charlie was mobilizing the guys for war, I came in and told everybody, "STAND DOWN." And they listened. Which had to be tough for most of them, because a lot of Ghetto Brothers were ready for war, they wanted to go war. But instead of war, I made a call for peace, and the GBs listened and backed me. Black Benjie's murder created a lot of transition between all the gangs in the Bronx. And I wanted to use the opportunity to make peace.

•••

The peace meeting, which became known as the Hoe Avenue Peace Meeting, was held the next week on December 7th, at 174th Street and Hoe Avenue, at the Boys Club. That was the name, Madison Square Boys Club. Oh, my goodness, that's were you seen the meanest gangs, they were all over there. And there was a lot of colors back in the days. Still, we proved to the world that these blacks and Puerto Ricans aren't a bunch of savages.

When I went up there to the peace meeting and I walked up the block, I see all these newspaper guys, all these reporters. I'm looking at them and they stood there with their pens ready to quote me. I could hear them saying, "That's him! That's him!" Then one of them said, "You're the leader here, huh?" Technically, I was the Vice President at the time, but I was still recognized by everybody as the leader of the Ghetto Brothers. The reporter says, "What are you going to do?" I looked at him, my eyes got watery. Every newspaper was there, The *Times*, the *Post*. And I said, "Nothing. Stand down." The guy says, "What?! OH, COME ON, BENJY?"

You can see that they were disappointed. They wanted a different story. They wanted to report on war and revenge and the black and Puerto Rican savages of the South Bronx. I told them, "No. Guys, listen to me: I lost my friend. I made him into a peace ambassador, a peacemaker. Declaring war is not going to bring my friend back…back to life. And I don't want his name to be in dirt. I'm going to honor his name by doing a peace treaty." Another reporter said, "No, Benjy, this can't be possible. How can you say that? You're breaking the rules." "I'm breaking the rules? I just lost my brother. I lost him. He lost his dreams. He will never have a wife, he will never have children. He's gone! No! I'm not going to lose no more Ghetto brothers."

One Ghetto Brother walks right by me while I was talking to the newspaper guys and said, "Benjy, I'm gonna go over your head." I told him, "NO! You're not gonna go over my head. It's bad enough I want you happy with your parents, with your girlfriend, to see another day.

Brothers, the violent cycle has to stop TODAY! Look at these newspapers. They're not writing. They want to tell the world that we are monsters! That we are Savages. They think we're savages. That we're not people who can think, that we can't reason. Let's show them that we are people, too. Let's show the world that we can reason in the midst of all this hate. Among all these burning buildings, the destruction of our community, the poverty, the neglect by city governments that don't care about us. We have to care for ourselves!"

Later on, 'cause I caught them newspaper guys off guard, then they started to write. I said, "See, brothers, they're not writing, 'cause they want promotions. They wanna tell the world a different story, they want the headline to be, 'We were in the thick of the violence.' That's the story they're here to cover."

Cops from all of the precincts in the Bronx were ready for the biggest war. There was so much tension in the air. But the war never happened. We got all of the major gangs of the Bronx together to discuss peace. This was the biggest peace meeting of the gang era, not just in the Bronx, ALL of New York City.

I didn't want a war. Even before my brother Black Benjie was murdered, people were coming up to me in those days saying, "Benjy, man, I don't wanna die." And after Black Benjie was killed, some leaders were coming up to me saying, "Benjy, please, man. I don't wanna die." I told one of the gang members involved in killing Benjie, "You're not gonna die, my brother. I'll let you know right now: I lost my brother. You hear me? I lost my brother. But you're not gonna die. You know why? 'Cause I said the Ghetto Brothers are not gonna do this."

But still, there were some Ghetto Brothers who didn't agree. Some GBs wasn't with the peace. They wanted revenge; they wanted to go to war no matter what I said. But ultimately, they listened and they backed my decision. And I loved them for that. "Benjy, we would've been in the history of the Bronx," a lot of the guys said. And I said, "Oh, see, it's a bunch of savages, right? You wanna be infamous? Or do you wanna be famous? You wanna be famous, then you gotta do the right thing. You wanna be infamous, go on with the category of Hitler! I don't wanna be known for that. With our parents, and when our children are suffering in this community, we're gonna go out and take more lives, man? THIS is what they want! This is what this corrupt government wants. This is what the people who hate us want. They WANT us to destroy ourselves and make their job easier. The police could simply say, 'We don't have to do nothing. Stay in your cars, stay in the precinct; let them kill each other. We'll go over afterwards and pick up the garbage.'" So a lot of the GBs did not like that I called for peace. But they went along with it, and there was no war.

Outside of the meeting, there were sniper cops, cops everywhere. You could see them on the rooftops. Inside the peace meeting you could feel the hostility in the air. A lot of tension. The whole thing almost unraveled because a lot of gangs in there had beef with each other. LOTS of unsettled scores, you know. All the leaders of all the major gangs were inside the meeting.

The meeting itself was like two or three hours long, because people had to vent. Savage Skulls venting, the

Savage Nomads venting, the Turbans venting. So I said, "Let them say whatever they want. Don't stop them. Just let 'em get it out." And you could see the anger, you could see it. And they all had the same ending, "Aw, man, but Benjy's my boy!" You know. "Charlie's my boy." "Yo, man, we gotta stop this. If it wasn't for the Ghetto Brothers, I would've shot you in the head!" You could hear that.

And I remember at the start of the meeting when Charlie said, "I don't want no cops here." And then, there was this guy with a camera, posing as a reporter. But he was really an undercover cop. That guy was a cop, too. And though there was a lot of hostility and anger in the room, no fights broke out. But you could definitely feel the anger and the tension in the air. A LOT OF TENSION. I was looking around at everybody. Because my fear was that somebody would sneak in a gun in and try to assassinate me or something. Then ALL HELL breaks loose!

But as the meeting went on, you could feel it fading. You could feel the mood change after Hollywood spoke. Hollywood was a Savage Skull, a black brother. When he spoke, things got really tense, but they calmed down after he started to talk about how the real problem in the community wasn't the gangs. Hollywood and I had spoken before, and I told him to look at what the real problems were in the community and why we needed peace.

Charlie and I were the first ones to speak. We were the ones who introduced the other gang members. And I was the one who called the peace meeting, so I had to play that role. Everybody expected that of me. You could feel my passion. The Ghetto Brothers knew me. All the gangs knew me. They already know how Benjy is. If you want Benjy, each club knew, if you want Benjy to come here, take one of his boys' colors. He'll come personally to get it. He doesn't come with his boys. I was known for that. No, I went by myself 'cause I didn't want nothing to happen to my guys. "All right, guys, can I have my colors back?" "You know, Benjy, if we want to, we can kill you." "Yeah, you can do that. But you're gonna have a lot of gangs coming down on you." This was understood about me. That's why I was the one who could call the peace meeting.

I earned my reputation. People knew they could talk to me, make peace, you know. But at the same time, people respected my power and my ability to fight. They used to call me "Legs." Some people at one time called me crazy, too. I was really fast with my legs. And I was good with my hands. So, I used it when it was necessary, when I was being threatened in some way. For example, there was these two gang guys in my club. I saw the American flag, this is when I was going through my Puerto Rican nationalist phase, I said, "Ay, I don't want that flag in here. Get it out of here." So my brothers Robert and David were coming up the block, and the only thing they remember is they saw a guy flying, 'cause I kicked him upside his head, BOOM! Remember, that's when we were in the transition from the Ghetto Brothers gang to the organization. Later on I said, I can't be doing that because I'm hurting one of my brothers. So I told the Ghetto Brothers, "Don't go there. It's stupid." I was wrong and I knew it. And I didn't want them following some stupid idea.

Even before the big peace meeting, I had already started talking peace. We were already talking peace.

Charlie and I started sending out Ghetto Brothers, scouts to go talk, "Ay, Savage Skulls, Ghetto Brothers are gonna have a meeting." "Turbins, Ghetto Brothers are gonna have a meeting." "About what?" "About the death of Black Benjie. Because this has got to stop." So this went on. Each gang started to talk to each other. And that's when we met at the Boy's Club.

But most of the real peace work got done after the peace meeting, behind closed doors. The city was trying to direct that meeting at the Boys Club. We didn't want the city to be there. We wanted the meeting to be one on one! So Charlie and I took the leaders from each club, we'd take them to United Bronx Parents, so we'd iron out our differences there. "Yo, well, why didn't you say that when—" "No, no, no! I didn't want to say that because there were cops there. That's none of their business."

For example, we didn't want altercations. We wanted gangs against gangs to settle things between each other hand to hand, one guy against one guy; that's all we need. Cops don't need to know our business. And then also, you can't do this, you can't point, you can't tell the cops nothing 'cause it's none of their business. We said, if you have any beef, don't tell the cops. Because all you're doing is ratting. When we can deal with it ourselves. We were young boys and we thought, why don't the people in the United Nations do the same thing? We did it.

With the black and Puerto Ricans, there was unity there, you understand. So we created a sort of system amongst the gangs and a new code for dealing with differences between gangs that limited the violence and the spread of street war. That was one of the outcomes of the peace meeting and the peace treaty that all the gangs signed.

• • •

When we initiated the peace treaty, over the course of time, people started dropping colors, little by little. When the Ghetto Brothers started taking off their colors and the berets were coming up, people were doing this: "Black Power!" "Puerto Rican Power!" People started doing the flags. The Puerto Rican flag, the Black Power flag, on the side of their jackets. So those who wanted to remain gangs, they felt more isolated, because there were more guys who wanted to get into an organization. And there were more guys who didn't want to live the gang life anymore. Some brothers joined the Young Lords, some brothers joined the Black Panthers; some joined the Ghetto Brothers Organization. Some people left altogether, joined the army. Some died, some went to jail. The gangs didn't immediately disappear. You still had gang violence in '72, '73. But the path was set by that monumental peace meeting. So while gang numbers continued after the treaty, the seed had already been planted. More and more people started shedding their colors. That's the real reason why by the end of the 1970s, the gangs weren't as big and wild as they once were; the peace meeting put that in motion. That would have NEVER happened if it wasn't for the peace meeting! What would've happened if I said let's go to war? What would New York City have been like now? The gangs would've just went on as is.

But after the peace meeting, it all started to quail. A decade! That's it. After we put the peace meeting together, everything gradually declined. The peace meeting lead to the de-escalation of the gangs in the South Bronx and throughout New York City. This is the reason gangs aren't big in New York City anymore to this day. There was once a time where street gangs were EVERYWHERE in the Bronx. A decade after the Peace Meeting, the gang era was finished. It was over. You maybe had a couple hard heads still trying to make gangs happen here and there, but it was really over. That gang era was done. The Peace Meeting set that in motion. And after the Peace Meeting, we invited all of the gangs to come to our Friday night concerts.

After the peace meeting, things changed. You still had the gangs of course. But by 1973, the mid-1970s, you could see the change happening. I started seeing the evolution. People were dancing, more parties were happening, people were being more relaxed about turf. The chaos was still there. The poverty, the dope was still in the community. But you could still see a change.

So the Peace Meeting was really the trigger that started everything. When I called for peace, when we had the peace meeting, when the Ghetto Brothers started taking off their colors, it started a domino effect. All the gangs started to follow suit. People started traveling more to other people's turf, for parties, you know. We invited everybody to our street parties. The Ghetto Brothers band played, and we just wanted people to have a good time. That's the atmosphere that we wanted with our music and street parties.

I remember when the Black Spades came to visit us. They saw that we were welcoming a lot of people. *These guys are playing the music, everybody's involved.* So they wanted to bring that into their community. They wanted to bring that excitement into their community. *We don't have to come to the Ghetto Brothers, which is good, but we can do it over here.* That's the idea Afrika Bambaataa got when he saw our block parties. They saw tons of people. That's where they got the idea — from the GBs. And he took it to the point where to this day, everybody knows who Afrika Bambaataa is for music. But there was a spark, and the spark was the Ghetto Brothers. We were already doing the dance parties, the block parties, a couple of years before Kool Herc and Bambaataa started doing them. Remember, we were The Junior Beatles before that. We were already playing. And then the Ghetto Brothers band, 1971. The Ghetto Brothers were the precursors. We were rock 'n' roll, though; then we were soul, Latin, and funk. Every gang knew, Benjy likes rock 'n' roll. I wrote a song, "Benjy Likes Rock 'n' Roll." Every gang knew our music.

So when we did the music, Afrika Bambaataa and these guys took it a step further with the rap and the hip hop dancing. I didn't know what that was. When I saw them dancing, I thought it was the Pentecostal. Victor told me it was "hip hop."

I saw when hip hop and everything started. Hip hop didn't come directly from the gangs. I think it's wrong for anybody to say that it did. If you were in a gang in '70, '71, '72, '73, or whatever, you weren't talking no *hip hop*. Hip hop didn't come directly from the gangs. There weren't any gangs that split up to become a *hip hop* club. But the change in the gang culture, the evolution of things was happening at that time. The parties and stuff. Some books might say otherwise, some people might want to try and say that hip hop came from the gangs, or that I paved the way for hip hop, but that ain't exactly the case. I was there. I saw it! Hip hop didn't come from the gangs. Even before the Peace Meeting, we, the Ghetto Brothers band, were playing live in the street. Street parties, you know.

I will say though, it was the peace meeting that put things in a new direction. It was another chapter in the life that we can say, "Yo, man, what did you hear?" The Peace Meeting broke down barriers. Bam Bam — Afrika Bambaataa — was at the Peace Meeting. I know it had a big impression on him; he was young, I think 14 at the time. After the peace meeting, it was just easier for people to travel more safely to different parts of the South Bronx for parties or to see friends and stuff. This made for a more relaxed, more creative atmosphere. You still had to watch out, you know. The gangs didn't disappear yet. But people were able to move about more freely. And we were already having our Friday night street parties a couple of years before Kool Herc's first hip hop party in 1973.

My brother Victor he was great. He said, "Benjy, it's music. Don't you know it's music everywhere you go now?" I said, "Yeah, and guess what? Even before you had Herc over here in 1973, the Ghetto Brothers, the band, we were doing that already! We were already jamming in the streets, on rooftops, inviting people to come party with us. And prior to the Ghetto Brothers, we were doing it as the Junior Beatles! We were entertaining the streets. Happiness! The drums. Then we started throwing in the guitar, we started doing parties in the street. On 163rd Street we put our amps on the poles, on the light poles.

This was '70, '71, '72, Ghetto Brothers were playing out in the street. And then we would ask some gang members, "Why don't you come with some of your guys, we're having a party, a Ghetto Brothers party, and we want you to come along." See, despite any bad that I or any GBs did — and I don't excuse any bad or wrong that I've ever done — I had long cultivated our reputation for ambassadorship and peace, which is precisely why the Peace Meeting and the treaty happened in the first place. The Peace Meeting just opened things up even more. That was the catalyst that eventually led to the end of the gang era.

And it's crazy, you know, because I'm thinking about Black Benjie's favorite song. The main song that Black Benjie liked was "I'm Your Captain" from Grand Funk Railroad. "I'm your captain" — anybody who heard us sing that song thought it was about *me*. Whenever the Ghetto Brothers did that song, everybody thought that I was singing about me, that I'm your captain. Like I was saying that *I'm your captain*.

So we did that, we played Satana songs. We did a mixture of Sly and The Family Stone. Every Friday, people knew. We had a great time! We had a great, great time when we played and everybody partied together. That was the atmosphere, the party feeling we created that made people want to come out and dance and just have a good time. That's the same atmosphere that hip hop was in the beginning. If there had been a big war, the atmosphere would've been completely different, big time. The Peace Meeting helped relax a lot of stuff. Turf was still important, but as more and more people left the gangs and got into other stuff, music, art, literature, you could see things were changing. The Peace Meeting put all of that in motion, because people saw a different way.

Ted Gross was asked, "What do you think kept everybody calm at that meeting?" And he said, it was his workers. WRONG! That was our effort. We kept things calm at the peace meeting. WE did that! The Ghetto Brothers. WE did that. Their workers, Ted Gross's workers? Get out of here. They were scared to come around our block. You had Red, this guy name Red. These guys knew everything about gangs! I got something, it's a menu that I copied from Red. It looks like a birth certificate from the old days, under Mayor Lindsey. It tells you all the gangs that are on here, what the cops reported and what they did.

Ted Gross was the guy who ran Youth Services Agency during the time of the gangs, giving jobs to the leaders of the gangs. So, if you keep the leaders busy, the members will cool down. 'Cause the leaders are busy working. Well, we were in a film together, but I forgot what I said. But he said, "Benjy's ahead of his time." I'm thinking this was how everybody else was thinking. I wasn't even going there. Only later on, Ted Gross was killed. GBs came to me, "Yo, Benjy, Charlie…" "What happened?" "Ted Gross! They found him. They found him dead. They shot him in the head." So, we all put things together. Some people said he was embezzling money. We didn't know whether it was true or not, but they killed him. They found him with a bullet in his head. That's sad man. He was a nice guy. He was really good with me and Charlie. Cool guy. But his workers didn't have *anything* to do with keeping everybody calm at the peace meeting.

In the movie *Ain't Gonna Eat My Mind*, there's a clip of me talking to one of the brothers, one of the guys, another gang member, the President of the Seven Immortals. He had come up to me earlier before that. He said, "Benjy, I don't wanna die." You know why he said that? All the gangs were ready for the Ghetto Brothers to give the word! It was like we were in the coliseum. All the gangs were there. They were waiting for this. Despite the fact that the cops were there. That Boys Club was like a Coliseum to us. You know what people were waiting for? A thumbs down from me! Charlie wanted to go to war.

When the Seven Immortals came up to me and said, "They don't wanna die," their fear was, here's what they mean: That not only were they going to get killed, but that gang members were going to rush into peoples apartments, families' apartments, mothers and fathers, and kill them all! This is what they feared. If the gangs declare war on you, all the major gangs, your greatest fear is to run and hide. Don't go into your apartment, 'cause they're gonna kill you, your mother, your brother, EVERYBODY there.

There was a time, before I called the truce, that people thought that there was going to be war against the Seven Immortals, the Black Spades, and the Mongols, all three. And it wasn't the members, it was the leaders! We always believed — back in the day all the gangs — that if something jumped up, we always went to their leaders. "Yo, your boys are out of control." These were the three gangs responsible for Black Benjie's death.

I was mad and sad that my brother Black Benjie was killed. He was for peace. I wanted those who did this to pay for what they'd done. But my heart and my mind told me that peace was the way. By this time, all the gang stuff was getting to me. I didn't want to be a bad guy anymore. I know there were probably a lot of other guys that felt the same way that I did. Some guys loved that gang stuff, though. They lived for it, it's all they had, all they knew. But everybody, at some point, was scared of dying. I don't care how tough you were. This was a fact for everybody in those days. Maybe you didn't show fear in the streets — you couldn't. But every gang member in those days, at some point, was scared of dying. And I didn't want any more brothers dying. I didn't want to be about that, man.

The leaders of those three gangs were really responsible because the leaders are supposed to keep their boys in check, meaning if any gang comes around your territory, you're supposed to — like the Geneva Convention — grab the guys and take 'em to the headquarters of the President, like, "Yo, we got some Ghetto Brothers here." That's what you're supposed to do. But they took it upon themselves to do those biddings. Where were the leaders? Their brothers are in their turf while their boys are running amuck. Unfortunately, they didn't do that, and my brother Black Benjie was killed. I just couldn't do it anymore. Peace was the only way to go, the only way to try to move us all forward. So that's what I did. I wasn't trying to be a hero. I just wanted peace.

Chapter 11
Trauma

My father died when I was twenty. It was a big loss for me. Not too long after calling for peace with the big summit, he passed away. So in a very short period, Black Benjie, my friend and brother, was tragically murdered, and my father had died. My father was truly a great man. I learned so much from that man. He taught me so much. About life. About character. How to be a man. How you should try to be. How you should treat people. Love your neighbor. My father taught me all of that. I couldn't have been a leader of anything if it wasn't for my father.

Right before my father died, I tried one last time to speak to him about our faith. He still didn't want to talk directly about it. I told him what I had learned, that I knew we were Jewish, but he didn't want to talk to me about it. I said, "You know, Papi, I think, uh—" He just wouldn't talk to me about it. It hurt. My brothers said, "Leave Papi alone, already." I loved my father very much. So I never pressed it with him again. I felt really bad. My mother used to say, "You know, Benjy, your father's got a strange religion." My father used to say, "Oh, your mother's got a strange religion."

After the peace meeting, the Ghetto Brothers grew even bigger and my notoriety increased. But not everybody was happy with this. There were some drug dealers and other criminals who didn't like what the Ghetto Brothers were trying to do. They didn't like what we were about, you know, trying to change the community, get the drugs and stuff out of the community. And then, there was some gangs who didn't like what we were doing. There were some gangs who felt that the Ghetto Brothers were getting too big, getting too much attention. Remember, some gangs lived for that gang stuff, they didn't want peace. But we, the Ghetto Brothers, we were growing and that message of peace was spreading, and I was on TV shows, doing interviews, meeting with people in the community, doing what I could to change things for the better. But to some people, I was getting too big. And it wasn't long before somebody tried to kill me.

Each gang, back in the days, had their own version of Gestapo — spies. And their main function is to spy on other gangs, infiltrate them; do whatever the President wants them to do. They had to accomplish the task of doing what the President said. *We gotta get rid of this threat.* They would join the gang, make friends. Once they become a member, they would find out the address of this person or that person and do what they had to do.

So the Gestapo were also assassins. These assassins, their main job and function is to do whatever the President wants them to do. You're gonna kill this person or beat up this person — either or. So in my case, this guy, Israel, went through my ranks. I befriended him, you know. One day, the guys say, "Benjy, this guy wants to see you." I didn't have bodyguards, but I had a lot of Ghetto Brothers surrounding me at all times. I was the type that had to choose my friends very carefully. *Very carefully.* So I didn't hang around much. When I was in the club, I was like a kid there. But when I left, I always stood with one, two or three guys; that's it. And I didn't want no bodyguards, that's how I was. I said, "Guys, I appreciate that, but listen, I don't need bodyguards." They would say, "Nah, Ben, we're gonna look out for you, man. 'Cause you don't know who's out there." So I was like, "O.K., I understand."

So one of my boys introduced me to this guy, Israel. He said, "Ay, yo, Benjy, this guy wants to know if he can be a member of the Ghetto Brothers." I said, "Sure." But instead of going to one of the staff leaders, I took him in directly. So we became friends and we were talking. He said, "Oh, I live over here, and I noticed what you guys were doing over here with the community. Man, this cool. I'd like to be a member of this division right here."

So then, I brought him to my house. I fed him, I took care of him, I introduced him to my wife, to my friends. Six months passed by. Every other day, every other weekend he would knock on my door, "Benjy, can I...?" "Yeah, come inside, my brother. The door is open!" So we would just talk, have a good time. We were close friends.

One day, he knocks on the door, I'm sitting in my living room. I say, "Who is it?" "Israel!" "Israel, come in." But then when he walked in, I saw him looking at me. He was looking at me funny, and he closed the door slowly like he was nervous. Right away, I said to him, "Gestapo?!" He slowly nodded his head. And then he pulled out a gun, a .45. I looked to my right where my samurai sword was. But I knew I couldn't reach it in time; I couldn't do anything anyway. So I just threw my hands up. And then he put the gun on my table and he started to cry. He says, "I can't do this, man. I can't do it. Man, you've been too nice to me. You've been really good to me. You treated me like a brother. You even allowed me to come here and eat in your own house. I can't do this." I said, "What gang do you represent?" He said, "The Bachelors." Those guys were bad, they were on Jackson Avenue. And they were the Bachelors when I was a Savage Nomad. They allowed some of my boys to occupy their space, they didn't mind, on Jackson Avenue. So the Bachelors had sent Israel to my house to assassinate me. But he didn't do it.

After that day, he left the house. He took the .45, went back to The Bachelors, and this is him telling me, he told them, "Listen, you told me to get rid of this guy? I can't do that. This is not the guy you think he is." They did that because I had a big group. They wanted me dead! The Ghetto Brothers was growing bigger, we were influential all over the Bronx. So they didn't like the fact that we were getting a lot of attention in the media, or that a lot of people liked us, or that people in the community supported us. And as a result of that, you get people in the community who wanted to join your organization even more.

So they wanted to get me out of the way because they were thinking, *If the Ghetto Brothers start getting too big, they're gonna take care of business with us.* And I said, "That's not what we're about. We're not here to conquer anybody. We're not a gang anymore. If I can inspire you to join me, with love and kindness for people, then I win you over." I remember giving this rich feeling to my boys. But there were some who didn't want to go for that. Some Ghetto Brothers wanted to leave when the organization period started. I remember one Ghetto Brother saying to me, "Yo, Benjy, I don't want to be part of this organization, I want to keep the outlaw look. Can I join the Savage Skulls?"

I told him, "It's up to you, my brother. I won't force you." Remember, in the old days, you gotta get initiated before you leave. But I didn't do that. I didn't make anyone go through anything like that if they wanted to leave. I said, "Man, you serious? I'll tell you what: The door's always open, you can come back any time."

That's the freedom I gave to my boys. Anybody who still wanted to fly colors and live that gang life, I just let them go. Some of them left and became Savage Skulls, Savage Nomads, Dirty Dozens. But even when they were in those gangs, they told their guys, "The Ghetto Brothers is not the way you think it is, man. That's why I left to be with you guys. The Ghetto Brothers are really cool guys, man, but that's not me. I wanna wear colors!"

You know, so, after that day, when Israel came to murder me… Oh, man, I remember the day. This was 1973. So Israel finally comes back, and we became the best of friends. This was two years after the peace meeting. And then after that, we were working together. I was his counselor at United Bronx Parents, he was a worker there. And we stayed close. Later on in the years, he became one of the bodyguards for Mayor Dinkins. Then after that, he became Vice President of the COs, you know, New York City Corrections Officers. He became big time, man. And he always called me. He always called me. Now he lives in Florida.

But before that, in those days, the kids that I was counseling, they got together and bought me the Torah. I have it to this very day; from the '70s to now. So I was talking to him one day when we were older, I said, "Israel, when you come down here, I want you to sign it." "You still got it?" "Yes, I still got it." When anybody gives me something, I hold it, I don't throw it away. I don't do things like that.

So look at the impression that I have given him. When he came over, he looked at my wife, Wanda, and says, "Wanda, I don't know you, I know MayLin, Benjy's first wife. But after all these years, this man has not changed. He is still the same guy." If you talk to gang members — Blackie, from the Savage Skulls, Ben Buxton, the other Black Benjie, from the Savage Nomads, *Tell me about Benjy? Benjy's always like that. Aw, man, Benjy's ALWAYS been like that*. Because that's the reputation I carry. But yeah, I forgave Israel. I understood. That was the price that came with being the President, the leader of the Ghetto Brothers. There were some people who wanted me dead.

• • •

After the peace meeting and the Ghetto Brothers transition, people trying to kill me wasn't the only thing I had to deal with. The growth of the Ghetto Brothers, the work that I was trying to do and all of the notoriety I got caused problems between my first wife, MayLin, and me. We were deeply in love, me and MayLin. She lived on 158th Street and Trinity Avenue. Man, she was such an artist. You know the album *Ball of Confusion*? She did a duplicate of the cover of that album. She was a great artist. That was one of her favorite songs. And her favorite group was The Supremes. So she used to draw. I said, "Hey, MayLin, what's that?" "Oh, that's *Ball of Confusion*." She drew the whole thing. It was fantastic. She was a great artist. She was never involved with the gangs. She didn't like the idea of the gangs from the get go!

Her parents, well, her mother, didn't like me at all, 'cause I wasn't Chinese. She always looked at me and started talking Chinese whenever I was around. I met MayLin on 158th Street and Trinity Avenue. One day, we were walking by, my friend Raymond and I. Remember, Raymond, that's the one who was living in the streets and my father took him in. So Raymond and I met her, and we're just talking, you know, small talk, nothing big. Then, originally, I went out with MayLon, MayLin's older sister. Raymond went out with MayLin initially. But one day, Raymond and I got together, I said, "Aw, Raymond, why don't you take MayLon and I'll take MayLin." He said, "O.K." So we switched MayLin. I said to MayLin, "I wanna be with you." And Raymond said to MayLon, "I wanna be with you." And I took MayLin. We were young. We were young kids.

So MayLin was one of those women that were stable, she had foundation. She was smart. She was Southern Chinese, what people would say, she's flat, you know. Whereas the Northern Chinese are more round. Their features come out a little more. Southern Chinese are smaller.

MayLin was a very nice person. Very pretty, long hair. Very intelligent, she knew three languages — Chinese, Spanish, and English. She was raised in a Puerto Rican community, so she knew how to speak Spanish and things like that. MayLin had more stability. So if she didn't like something, she'd let you know it immediately. That's how she was. And she was adamant about it, "I don't like it, and you ain't going, that's it! And you ain't going there." I was alive because of that lady right there. I told my son, "Your mother, if it wasn't for your mother, I would've been dead." She kept on telling me — there was times you know, women's premonition. She'd say, "Benjy, don't go there. I sense something bad is going to happen." EVERY time she said that, something very bad happened. She always told me, "I don't like the idea of you wearing those colors." Funny thing, she actually helped me paint them, we painted them together, the original Ghetto Brother colors. So every time I wore that, something happened.

You know, even though the daily life of being in a gang, being in the streets, took a toll on me, I didn't always feel depressed or hopeless. I was still happy because I had a family. I had a mother, I had a father, we always had food. This wasn't the case for most Ghetto Brothers and other gang members. When we were on "The David Susskind Show," and there were the leaders of the gangs around in semi-circles, and David said, "Oh, a lot of these people live in single parent homes." "Not Benjy. Benjy has a mother and father." He says, "What?!" I said, "Yes, I have a mother and father."

Some kids in gangs had both parents. But most of the kids had single parents, mother, grandmother, aunt, you know. In my family, every time we want to sit, my father had us together. And you know what was the best part, is when we would have our Bible studies. We used to sit together, even in those gang days. Remember, my parents didn't know I was in a gang. I would put the colors away before I went home. I'd go home, take a bath. I was ready. And I would invite some of my friends over and tell them, "hide your colors." So they knew my father for that. My father was a good host. He would treat people well. I would say, "Poppy, this guy's gonna come." He'd happily say, "O.K., let them come." So we would sit there, and friends of mine would look and say, "Yo, man, I like this family." So then one Ghetto Brother said, "That's the way Benjy treats us. He thinks that, you know, we're his family." "You *are* my family," that's what I would say. "I'm treating you the way my parents treated me."

So I would smile. But if I was ever too depressed or sad or jealous, it was because of MayLin. "What are you doing looking over there?" when she really wasn't. I was just, remember, I was young. I was a virgin when I met her. We were both virgins. When I first got married, I didn't know what to do. I had to ask Charlie. "Charlie, what-a-you do?" You see what I'm saying? For these things, you wasn't taught that in the home. My parents were from the old school, you don't talk about that. It has to come natural. When I went to my mother to talk about it, my mother looked at me, she said, "What happened?" I said, "Ah, nothing," and I just walked away. She knew that I wanted to talk about something. I was like, "Uh, uh…," I was real nervous. I couldn't go to my father. So my mother was laughing and my sister was giggling. So I said, "Oh, boy…"

So I went to Charlie. I said, "Charlie, what-a-you do?" So he described it to me. I said, "Hey, yo, Charlie, that sounds disgusting!" He said, "WELL, THAT'S WHAT YOU GOTTA DO!" So then I asked, "How do you have a baby?" "Well, Benjy, you do this and this, and both of you's have to *come* together." "*Come* together?

WHAT-A-YOU MEAN?" I didn't know, I didn't know ANY of these things. Look at me: I'm flying colors, the President of one of the biggest gangs in New York City, and I'm a virgin! I didn't know none of that stuff!

I didn't know none of that! I didn't know nothing about sex. And then girls would come up to me, back in the days, wanting to get with me, "Yo, Benjy…" I'd be like, "No, no, no, we can't do this. My girlfriend… I gotta go home 'cause my mother wants me." So girls got the idea, "Yo, I think Benjy's a homo." They didn't say gay in those days. So one girl said, "No, he's not. He's got MayLin." Then the other girls were like, "Ahhh…" So they knew I wanted to keep her true. They didn't know that I was a virgin. I didn't want no problems. My father had told me about gonorrhea and syphilis. Oh, no, no, I can't do that! And some of the guys were like, "Yo, Benjy, these girls…" "Nah, you take 'em. Not me."

So again, after the peace meeting, the Ghetto Brothers just started getting bigger, and bigger, and bigger. We had divisions all over the place. Now, according to my books, I had 2,000 guys in the Bronx alone. I was the one who kept record of that stuff. Blackie, every gang knew me. "But, Benjy keeps records…" I do, I keep records of everything. And I said, "Look, MayLin. Look at all these notebooks I got. Look!" And I counted 2,000 guys in the Bronx alone. And at the height of everything, we had Ghetto Brothers in all five boroughs. Plus, Pennsylvania, Connecticut, Chicago, and Puerto Rico. But this was later on, after the gang days, when we were a political organization. This was towards the middle to late 1970s.

We had gone way beyond the Ghetto Brothers that

we used to be, we went way beyond that. We transcended that and said, "No!" to a lot of that racial tension. If anything, anybody who lived in our community was part of the Ghetto Brothers. Whether you're black, Chinese, or white. I remember one time, I walked up in the Ghetto Brothers clubhouse and I looked across the street, it was in the morning, and I saw this white dude with a Lee jacket, Lee pants, with his hair combed back like *Westside Story*. Guy stood out like a sore thumb. And I'm looking at this guy. And I told the guys, "Yo, who's this guy?" "Yo, Benjy, he just moved in." So I walked across the street. I just walked up to him and was like, "Hi, what's your name?" "My name is Joe Heineman." "My name is Benjy, how you doing?" He said, "I know about you. I read a lot about you when I was in New Jersey. You guys are the Ghetto Brothers, right?!" "Yeah." "I came here because I wanted to join you guys." See, something good, something positive caused him to move from New Jersey to rent an apartment right here in the South Bronx. He wanted to be a member of the Ghetto Brothers.

So this was the climate after the peace meeting. People all around knew us. And because I was the leader, there were a lot of demands on me. After MayLin and I got married and after I got a lot of attention from leading the Ghetto Brothers education, things changed. When I was in the Ghetto Brothers, I spent a lot of time with the GBs, a lot of time. I spent so much time that women get lonely, wives get lonely. They want their husband. Where's their husband? I was in meetings and more meetings. Interviews, more interviews. Television, radio. I was always out. And while I was out trying to save the community, she was falling out of love with me. I still loved her deeply, but she was falling out of love with me.

And then, I looked at her one time and said, "MayLin, what's happening?" She didn't wanna do nothing with me; she didn't want to make love with me anymore. She wasn't as close to me as I thought I was to her.

I remember my father once told me, "Don't bring your friends to your house. 'Cause if they come to your house, they're not coming to see you. They're coming to see your wife." I didn't pay no mind to those words when my father told me. Well, my best friend kept on coming around. Then one day, I felt suspicious. I'm coming home on 162nd Street, I go to the basement. I go around — MayLin and I lived on the first floor — I looked in the window and I saw MayLin hugging my best friend, Cokie. I went into the building, I opened the door from the basement, go to the first floor, knocked on the door. It opens up. I looked at him, "Yo, what's going on over here, my man?!" This was my right hand man! He was a Ghetto Brother. I said, "What are you doing?!" I look into the apartment, to my left and I saw my samurai sword. I said, "Yo, are you doing something with my wife over here?!" One of my boys was coming over. I go into the apartment. MayLin said, "No, No, Benjy!" I grabbed the sword, ready to chop him up. My boy, another GB, grabs me, throws me on the floor. Cokie runs out! I said, to my boy, "Get off me!" And MayLin started to say something. I told MayLin. "SHUT UP! What's going on over here?!"

She was with the guy! She straight up told me that she was with the guy. That's one thing about her: She'll tell you straight. Chinese are not like these people out here.

They'll tell you. She said, "You wasn't with me. That was my lover."

That was my lover. That's what she said. It CRUSHED me. For the first time in my life, I started drinking. For the very first time! I wanted to get this out of my mind. I was going crazy. I was crying. Everyday, I was crying. We had a little girl. I was holding her, I was crying, *Oh, my goodness. What I'm gonna do?* And the Ghetto Brothers. You know, word gets around. "Yo, what's happening over here, man?" And the guys had started to look at me. You know, word gets around! "Man, what's happening? No, no, no, Benjy—" And I was so angry, because she kept on seeing him.

This guy was one of my boys. He was one of my right hand men. He used to stay in my apartment. I fed him. I gave him food stamps. We we're close. I looked out for him. But he just did not take the food stamps or the help or the friendship, he took my woman! That was my first wife. I was a virgin with her!

"What are you doing?!" I'm saying to MayLin, you know what I mean? And here I am, I'm going mad. I'm going out of my mind. I didn't wanna see the Ghetto Brothers. I just wanted to be by myself. And I used to cry for any little thing.

1974! I remember looking at her and asking, "MayLin, did you do something with him?" "I did." "Come on, MayLin you gotta be kidding!" She said, "Yeah." And I looked at my daughter. That was my only consolation, my daughter. I would dress her up and take her out for a stroll. I was really sad. I'd take my daughter to Hunts Point. And there was a little cemetery there. I would sit there and cry, just cry. 'Cause I said, "Who can do this?! How can you do this to me, MayLin?!" "You wasn't there, Benjy." That was her only answer. NO! I couldn't believe that she did that to me. I couldn't believe that MayLin could ever do that to me. I was true to her. I remembered what my father said, "If you're gonna do something, give me a divorce, then do what you have to do." Don't do it while we're married!

It was such a trauma to me in those days that I still have dreams to this very day, about what MayLin did. To this very day. I still hear her voice. I still see everything. In my dreams, I'm reliving the whole thing over again. And one day, I got upset with Wanda, my second wife. You know what, she looked at me and said, "You get a good look at me, Mr. I am not this woman! I'm your wife. I would NEVER do to you what she did to you. Don't treat me like I'm her. This is a marriage of two people. I'm married to you. What she did to you, I am really sorry, Benjy. But now, I have you. I'm taking care of you. I'm loving you. I do EVERYTHING for you. Let that woman's past die!" I said, "Wanda, I want to. But it's here, it's seared in my head!." It's a trauma that I can never forget.

One day, aw, man, I remember, back before all this happened, Franky, another GB, came up to me. And I remember, we were at a party on 158th Street, my 2nd division. "Hey, Benjy. You got married to MayLin, right?" I said, "Yeah." He said, "How is it?" He said, *"How is it?"* I said, "What? What do you mean? What are you saying to me? How is *what*?" And he says, "You know, the sex?" BOOM!!!! I punched him right in the mouth, broke his tooth. We were in his mother's house; his mother came out. I told her the whole story. She said, "No, no. I'm sorry." She looked at her son and said, "That's good. That's what you get for asking a stupid question." And I told him, "You know what? You're outta here, buddy. No more GB. You're outta here!"

Franky knew MayLin before me, because they had the Chinese laundry downstairs. He said, "How is it Benjy. Is it like this or like this…?" Can you believe that? You don't do things like that, man. All the Ghetto Brothers looked at me, "Benjy, what do you want us to do, Benjy?" "Don't do nothing. I don't want you to do anything. Franky, you're outta of the GBs." "Yo, Benjy, I'm sorry." "I don't wanna hear it." I never told MayLin what he said, 'cause his sister was MayLin's best friend, so I didn't wanna break that up. So I kept it to myself. I said, "Franky, you're outta here." So the Ghetto Brothers said, "Yo, Benjy, let's finish the job, we'll do it right here." "No, this is his mother's house. How you gonna do something stupid?" They said, "Aw, O.K.…Yo, Franky, don't hang around us, man. You just ruined it, big time!" You don't say things like that to your brothers, to your friends. Ghetto Brothers looked at me carefully, because Franky was my right hand man at that time. Wherever you saw me, you saw him. So when you do something like that, what do you think is going on in the minds of all the Ghetto Brothers?

MayLin and I tried to work it out. We talked to a minister. Me and MayLin went to a marriage counselor. You know what the minister said? He said, "MayLin, Benjy will forgive you. He's not gonna forget. He's not gonna forget!" Even after going to the marriage counselor, she didn't want to have sex with me. So things changed for me too. One day, I'm looking at the television and she comes in wearing a nice negligee. I said, "MayLin, I'm trying to watch a program." She said, "Benjy!" I said, "I'm trying to watch a program. I don't wanna have nothing to do with you." I can't do it. I couldn't see myself touching her anymore. Somebody was inside of her that wasn't supposed to be. She was my wife. She had no business doing that! The anger was in me so much that I couldn't take it.

I'm a very compassionate person. And I was a young guy. Before that, she wanna have sex? I'm there! Even when I wanted to do something with her, she didn't want to. "MayLin, please. Let's do something." She would take a bath. And I would give her a rub. She'd say, "Put cream on me." And I'm sitting there, and I'm thinking, I'm ready to roll! She says, "O.K., I'm going to sleep." DAMN! I had no idea why she didn't want to make love to me anymore. I had no idea that it was because she had a lover. And it was one of my boys!

So, she'd go to sleep and I would leave the apartment, take the train down to 42nd Street and go to the booths in Times Square; the ones where you could look at the women. I started doing that. I said to myself, let me do this so I won't be with another woman, let me do this. And whenever I came out, I started to cry. One time, one of the ladies from the booth comes out. She looks at me and says, "You're married, right?" I says, "I am." She said, "She broke your heart, right? She did something?" "Yeah." "You don't belong here. You're a handsome young man. You can get any woman out here." This is what she's telling me. "You don't need to do this. This is gonna drive you crazy," she says. And it was driving me crazy.

My feelings and love for MayLin was waning. I wrote a song about it:

I was so in love before, but my heart has died and co-o-old/ She played so many games with me/I was blind, I couldn't see/ You see, I really loved that girl/Until I felt this feeling deep inside, she was not all there/I lived in a fantasy, thinking she's the one for me/When I get to real-ize, my whole world was upside down/I had to run away from her/I had to run away and find some love in a world of loneliness.

That was her impact on me. How could she do that to me? She knew what I was doing out there with the Ghetto Brothers. I was trying to bring the community together, I was trying to save the community, make a better place for her, me, everybody. I was trying to stop the gang violence! I was trying to clean up the dope! I was trying to help people eat! And when I come home to be with the one I love, you're coming with this excuse, "Oh, you wasn't with me, so I'm going to do this." Come on, lady! It's called patience. Be kind to me. I'm coming home to you! I'm not going anywhere else.

And the girls, the girls, when they found out, they felt really sad. "Yo, Benjy! Yo, man, what MayLin did?! Not cool, man." But who I really had to watch was the guys. Remember, she was Chinese! She was not Puerto Rican. So they were curious.

Some Ghetto Brothers said to Cokie, "Yo, man, what you did, what you did to Benjy, yo, you lucky Benjy didn't put a cross around your neck. You lucky! 'Cause if Benjy would've gave the command, you would've been a dead man." I didn't want to kill him, I didn't want to have the guys kill him. I was done with it. We were an organization. I was done with the violence. And even though he did that to me, I was done with the violence. We were not a gang anymore. But I kicked Cokie out of the GBs, oh, yeah, for sure! "You've been gone! You're banished," I told him. "If you see me walking here, go to the other side." Look, I'm a very compassionate person. I love people. But he really crossed me. But I couldn't bring myself to give the order to kill him. I didn't want that, 'cause it wasn't in me. I wasn't going to have that on my conscious. It's bad enough that the adultery was committed, and now murder? Remember King David? When he saw this woman? He committed adultery, with who? He committed adultery with the wife of his general, one of his best men. He had him murdered! *I don't want him to know that I'm screwing his wife, so let's plan something to get him killed.* And God said, "What did you do? It's bad enough you commit adultery. You had to kill her husband, too?" So that's why I couldn't kill Cokie.

After that, when that situation happened. I prayed. "God, give me a son." I thought that having another baby would bring us close again. So MayLin gave me a son. But the feelings were still not there. My love for my son was stronger than for her. I kissed him more than I ever kissed MayLin. She already knew. MayLin told her friend, one of my 7th Division Ghetto Brothers, one of the presidents of the 7th Division, his wife. MayLin tells her, "I don't think Benjy sees me like that anymore." Remember, the news already got around. "He doesn't see me the same way anymore." Put yourself in my shoes. She was my diamond. The only one who could look at that was me!

The only who could go in there was me! Somebody else was in there. DON'T COUNT NO MORE! I don't see you the same way anymore. Nah! And then one day I said, "MayLin, I'm going to find me somebody out there." You know what she said to me? She said, "You're not man enough to leave me for another woman!" 'Cause she knew I was madly in love with her. But I did leave. Remember the song, "By the time I get to Phoenix?" Listen to that song. That's me! And then the ending, "She will never know, I will really go." She never knew that I was gonna go. But I left.

In 1975, that's when we broke up. But before we broke up, she had been telling me, "I want you to leave the Ghetto Brothers, Benjy. I don't want a hero. I don't want an icon. I want you. I want my husband. You don't sleep with them, you sleep with me. I'm having your baby, so I'm gonna give you an ultimatum: Either you leave them, or I'm going to leave." So I said, "I'm not going to leave you, May-Lin." So I went down the hill to the Ghetto Brothers headquarters. I said, "Guys, I got news." Everybody stopped. They said, "What is it, Benjy?" "I quit." "NO!!!!" Some guys were wailing, "No, Benjy… I bet you it was May-Lin," one of the GBs said. I said, "Watch it." "No, Benjy, man, 'cause she's too much of an influence over you." "But that's my wife." That night, she received a phone call: "You took away our leader, we're gonna take care of business with you." My wife received death threats, man! From some GBs. So it was 1975, that's when I quit the Ghetto Brothers. Because of the death threats and things, I packed up and moved my family to Jessup Avenue and 170th Street. I didn't tell nobody! Soon, there were rumors about my death.

•••

One day, about five years later after me and MayLin got divorced, my brother introduced me to the band that they were starting. My brothers were in the basement, I go down in the basement, who do I see sitting there? Wanda! She was wearing a white blouse, black dress. BEAUTIFUL! She's staring at me with big eyes. I said, "My goodness!" Remember, my heart and soul was always with MayLin. Victor said, "Benjy, this is Wanda." "Wanda, this is my older brother, Benjy." I took her hand, which I never did to no woman, and I kissed it. And I said, "Man!" I fell in love with her, right there, first sight! And I looked at her, and Manny, the bass player said, "Wanda, you gotta go." I said, "No, no, no, no. Sit down. You gotta stay. I'm gonna sing a song for you." I forget the name of the song I sang to her, but it was a Beatles song. From that day on, every time we went to the basement — Wanda lived upstairs — I invited her downstairs. 'Cause Manny used to teach her the bass. So we became friends. So wherever we went to play, Wanda came with me. This was around 1980, 1981.

From there on, I was with Wanda for like a whole year. Wanda was beautiful. Oh, my goodness. She was a mermaid. Face: BEAUTIFUL! Body: BEAUTIFUL! Wanda took a liking to me. She said, "I noticed you're so different from your brothers. You know, your brothers are very vulgar. Except your brother Victor." My brother Victor always showed respect to Wanda.

Finally, I looked at Wanda one time, and I said, "Wanda, I'm beginning to fall in love with you." She said,

"Aw, Benjy, I don't have feelings for you." I was hurt! This was a whole year. She never gave me a kiss. Never took my hand. But everywhere I went, I took her with me. Then as time went on, she was checking me out. And she found out that I wasn't what she thought that I was. My brothers vouched for me. My brother Victor said, "My brother, here? Nah, man, this guy's different from us. Benjy? True blue! Big time. Married, man. His wife did him wrong. If you're gonna go out with my brother treat him well, 'cause he has a broken heart. My brother has gone through hell." And then from there on, Wanda started to get close to me. Then one time she gave me a little kiss. *One kiss.* And then from there, two or three months down the line, I gave her an engagement ring. I proposed to her, and she accepted.

I introduced her to my mother. "Mommy, this is — in Spanish — Wanda." She looked at Wanda and said, "She's beautiful!" She thought Wanda was Turkish. And then from there, everything was history. We got married. A private wedding. Then six children later, here we are.

And all during that time, the rumors were still flying around about my death. "Benjy died. And they killed him in jail." That's what people were saying. I met two guys on Webster Avenue and Tremont. They were in the grocery store. Wanda was standing over here, buying stuff. And I'm looking at them, these two Ghetto Brothers, older guys, talking about the Ghetto Brothers album and the gang. One says, "What division were you in?" The other says, "I was in the 13th division." "Oh, yeah, I was in the 4th division." So I'm looking at both of them, I say, "Excuse me, guys. Are you talking about the Ghetto Brothers?"

They both looked at me, "Yeah, what about it?" I said, "I heard a lot about them." One of them proudly said, "Aw, man, we did some good stuff, man. We took out the drugs, man, we cleaned our community, man." I said, "Who was the leader?" The guy got sad and said, "Yellow Benjy." I said, "What happened to him?" He said, "They killed him, man. I was in jail with him, man. Yeah, they hanged him. The cops hanged him. We had a great organization and they had to kill Benjy." And the other guy said, "Yo, they did, man?" "Yeah, man, I never forgot what they did to him, man. When they hanged him, he said, *'Viva La Puerto Rico!'* I couldn't say nothing 'cause there were cops around." So when they left, Wanda said, "Why didn't you say anything?"

But that's how it was. Lot's of people thought I died, that I was killed. There was this one time, a guy comes into my apartment, fixes the light fixture. And he stares at me and he looks at me long and hard and says, "Ay, I seen you somewhere before." Then he goes, "YELLOW BENJY! YO, BENJY! *I thought you was dead?!*" So he hugs me. He never told anybody. We're still in contact with each other. A lot of people thought that I died, that I was killed. Bam Bam, Afrika Bambaataa, thought I died; everybody thought I was dead.

There was another time, I was on Simpson Street, I was going up the stairs with my wife, Wanda, there was this guy, a cop, I remember from years ago from Fort Apache, his name is Medina. He looked at me, he said, "Are you Benjy?" And I said, "Yes. Oh, Medina?!" I recognized him. He said, "BENJY! *You're alive?*" I said, "Yes." And the cop next to him said, "You know this guy?" "Yes, oh, do I know this guy?!" And he shook my hand anyway. Then he said, "Benjy, I thought you were dead."

And Wanda was with me during those times. She was my friend, she knew everything. She understood why I wasn't interested in correcting the rumors. I love that woman. Wanda and me had six children together: John, Natalia, Rachel, Sarah, Zipporah, that's the name of Moses' wife, and my son Judah. I always wanted a lot of children. I love kids, I wanted to have a lot of kids because I came from a big family. Originally, there was 12 of us. But then there was only 8, because the other four died, three from complications at birth. And there was my little sister who died in that fire. So I had always wanted a big family. I knew it was gonna happen. I told Wanda I wanted more, but she said, "The factory's closed." I love that woman.

You know, a couple of years ago, we're older now, she looked at me a couple of years ago, and I looked at her and she said, "Benjy, you don't see me the same way." I said, "Wanda, I see you as if I met you just now. We've been together for 30 years. I love you more than I have ever loved any woman. There is not a woman that I thought that I could love more than MayLin. And it's you." And I began to sing to her, *"I give her all my love…"* Again, a song from The Beatles! *"That's all I do/And if you saw my love you'd love her too, I love her…* That song I dedicate to you, Wanda. You're my world. You're everything to me. When I was sick, you was there for me. When I was going through hell, you was there for me. When I was at my dialyses, everything."

Wanda helped me get past the trauma of MayLin. Wanda has treated me good to this very day. You know what that lady does? I could come home right now, two or three o'clock in the morning. I could come into the house, and she'd say, "Sit down, I'll make you food." "Wanda, I can do it." "No, no, no, no, I'll do it." In other words, she wants to cater to me. As tired as she is, she's still there for me. "You know why I'm doing that, Benjy?" she said. "Because you don't have to look this way, nor this way. You have everything you got right here. And then if it comes to doing anything, just say, 'I want to,' and I'm there. Even if I don't feel like it. 'Cause my duty is to make you happy."

When a woman talks like that and says, "You can have me, 24hrs a day. You can be sleeping, four o'clock in the morning, wake me up, and you wanna do something, let's roll!" I said, "Wanda, come on. You know how many friends I asked that. 'Man, my wife don't do things like that. I wish I had a woman who'd do that." I can be sitting there, and she goes like this, a lion, you know. I'm a lion now. She goes, "All right, let's talk. You wanna go now?" That makes me feel good. So in other words, I don't have to worry. No more token. No more going to 42nd Street. No more looking in magazines. I don't need it. I got it right there now. Before, I had to beg for it. MayLin, I had to beg for it. "Come on, MayLin, you just finished taking a bath. I just put cream on your leg, you say 'No!' Can you let me at least play? She said, 'No!'" That's when the heart becomes cold. Ice cold!

So put it this way. This is a product of what MayLin did. So much trauma she put on me, I thought that I could never love another woman and be happy again. So to this very day — MayLin died about 10 years ago — to this very day, it's never left! The trauma is still in my mind!

My son asked me — my son from MayLin — some years ago, "Papi, do you still have feelings for Mommy?" I said, "No, my son, I don't." He said, "I believe you now, Papi." I said, "I'm with Wanda, I have no time for MayLin. She's gone. The only thing I have is a bad memory. That's all." You know, if I see Cokie right now, my hair would stand up. Would I forgive him? I'll forgive him. But I won't associate with him. I don't wanna be around him. And when I think about everything that happened with MayLin, it reminds me that the trauma's still there, seared into my mind. But I have Wanda.

Part 5
The Hourglass

Chapter 12
Life After Ghetto Brothers

It's been years since I've seen anybody from back then. I haven't seen nearly any of the guys I used to roll with in the Ghetto Brothers, or any of the guys I was cool with from the other clubs. After MayLin received death threats, I vanished, I moved away and didn't tell nobody. But also, many guys never made it out of the gang era. Unfortunately, many were killed, ended up on drugs, went to jail. But a couple of guys maybe got a decent job, but not most.

Kayto is still around. Beast is still around, too. I have not seen Kong for the longest time. The last time we were together was in 1975, when the Ghetto Brothers band was up on the roof of 940 Tiffany, just playing music. And the song that he did was "It's Only the Horizon." It's one of his original songs. After that, I never saw him again. Franky is another guy. Franky I haven't heard from him. I haven't seen Dead Eye Freddy We called him that because he had one eye that was droopy.

Now, my ex-Vice President, Táto. He's still around, but he's dying of AIDS. And Joey Conzo took a picture of me and him. I said, "Joey, can you do me a favor? Take a picture of me and Táto before the guy goes." And Joey said, "Benjy, let me know, whenever you need the picture, I'll make a copy for you."

This is right after I started to learn this. I didn't know this. And now, later on after the Ghetto Brothers organization, Táto became like a male prostitute, man — going with girls here and there. And I saw him and said, "Damn, Táto?! What happened to you?" "Yo, Benjy, that's what I get for messing around with all those girls. I don't know if I got it by using dope, or maybe I contracted it from one of the girls I was with. But, I got it."

• • •

Even years after my father died, my mother still avoided talking about our faith. She just said one day when I brought my son over, he was wearing a kipa, she said, "Don't you dare let your son wear that! Take it off!" "But why, mommy? We're not in Spain." She said, "No, no, no, no. 'Cause something could happen to him." So to respect her, I took it off. She didn't want me to talk about that. Like my father, she was secretive even after all those years. Most Jews do things out in the open, but Moranos — secret Jews — don't do that. They hide. Everything is inconspicuous. A lot of Jews confronted me, "Well, why didn't you make a big thing out of it?" I said, "You're not in my shoes! You don't know."

But as an adult, I became less secretive about who I am. I made a point of that. There was this one time in 1979, I was at the 96 Street Y. So I'm sitting down and there's this woman. She sees all these Jews around her, and I'm the only one who looks different from everyone else. No blue eyes, no blond hair. And she looks at me and she says, in front of everybody, "What is your name?" And I said, in Hebrew, "My name is Benjamin." She said, "What's your last name?" I said, "Melendez." She said, "That's not Jewish." I said, "What's your last name?" She said, "Bernstein." I said, "That's not Jewish, that's German."

A Rabbi, I forget his name, a rabbi from Argentina, gets up and walks up to her, "Don't you know anything about Sephardic Jews?" The word Sephardic means Spanish. He said, "Don't you know anything about Spanish Jews? If anything, their culture is older than yours! And their rituals are much longer than yours. And if anybody speaks Hebrew, it's these people."

You know what's funny. I talked to all of them, I said, "If anybody who looked more Middle Eastern, it's me. You do not look Middle Eastern. You look more European. You were mixed." The Ethiopian Jews. You know what they consider themselves? The House of Israel. That's what they call themselves. I said, if you go to Israel today, most of the people have color.

•••

There was one thing about me that never changed after I quit the Ghetto Brothers. You know, something that's always stayed with me: My love for music! After the Ghetto Brothers band, Robert and Victor continued doing what they were doing. They were always together. They played with other bands. Rock was their thing, oh, yeah, yeah. That was their thing, boy. Well, they joined a hard rock band called Nebulous. My brother Robert joined first. Then he brought my brother Victor in. Then he got my cousin David into the band. So they sounded even better than the band that they had before. One day I said to them, "Hey, we used to play in the pass, we were brothers, why don't we start the band again?"

This was kind of how our band Street the Beat was

born. Me and Robert were working in Staten Island, putting swimming pools together. Management wanted to separate us. 'Cause, you know, they were like, "Nah, I don't won't two brothers working together. You work over here with this company. Benjy, you work over here." So you know what we did? I said, I don't wanna do this anymore. So we had our guitars in the back of the station wagon we drove to work. So we went for the first time to the Staten Island Ferry. And that's where we started to sing. And that was just me and Robert in the beginning.

This was before we started Street the Beat. I said to Robert, "What can we call ourselves, a name of the band that's very synonymous to Ghetto Brothers?" He said, "Street." So that's what we went with, just "Street." Then, we met this guy Richard Alexander. Later he became our manager. He said, "Hey guys, what's the name of the band." We said, "Street." He said, "I'm gonna add, 'the Beat.'" I said, "What?!" He said, "Come on, guys. It's gonna stick." And it did. So the name of the band became Street the Beat. We became favorites in the West 4th Street/West Village area.

It was 1980 when we officially started Street the Beat. I'd left the pool job in Staten Island, and I went back to UBP, United Bronx Parents, they had rehired me. So me and Robert said, "Let's make money by doing this." So we started playing more regularly, taking it serious, making lots of money playing in the street.

With the cops, everything with us was diplomacy. Sometimes they'd be like, "Guys, you can't play here." All right, so we'd moved to another place. We looked for strategic areas. We were at WOR — WOR radio.

So the guy asked us on the radio, "Why do you call it 'strategic areas?'" "'Cause that's the place where you make money. You make money on 72nd Street and Columbus or Broadway, West 4th Street." So we would go to places where we knew we could generate money.

We were able to make a lot of money doing this. There were great times. Every Saturday. We would be walking to a spot to perform at and Victor would drag his makeshift drums. His make-shift drums consisted of two milk crates (one to sit on and one in front of him), two sticks, a tambourine, a cow bell, and a juice box. The box had to be Tropicana, 'cause it has a good solid sound. And then the bass had to be Charmin toilet paper. Victor was a professional drummer, but this is what we did. Instead of him trying to bring his real drum set around, he brought these makeshift drums. It was easier, more mobile. We were like The Little Rascals. So instead of walking down the street with a set of drums, we made our own drum set. And every band that used to know us said, "Man, you guys are geniuses! Homemade drums!"

We were offered good stuff when we became Street the Beat. Ghetto Brothers were O.K. when it came to making money. Aside from our album, our opportunities as the Ghetto Brothers band were O.K. But when we became Street the Beat, playing around in the West Village, we made money. West 4th Street, Sheridan Square. Right up the block, William Morris Agency, the guy threw his card into our hat. And then Sid Bernstein — the guy who brought The Beatles over to America — in the beginning he didn't want us; he dismissed us. He heard the songs, he said, "Who's song is that?" The song was, "I'm Not That

Crazy Over You." I said, "It's me." He said, "I like the way you sound there. I tell you what guys, why don't you sing in front of the Art Museum. You'll probably make some money." He dismissed us!

Two, three months down the line, Peter Halpern got us some gigs, we were all over the newspapers. Then Bernstein actually called us, we said, no! Other people wanted our songs, too. Joan Jett, she wanted "Crazy Boy," a song that we did, me and Victor collaborated. "Crazy Boy" was about me. She wanted that song. And Melenkamp, John Cougar Melenkamp, he wanted that song, too. We said, no. Because Peter Halpern, our manager, told us, "If you sell him the song, it's not yours anymore." So Victor said, "Nah, nah, forget it! It's my song. I ain't gonna give that up." So we let them down. This was around 1982.

Street the Beat was fun! One time, we appeared on "Good Morning America" with Regis Philbin. What happened is that we were all over the newspapers. So he inquired about us, he wanted to know who these guys are that they're playing all over the place and they're getting into the news. We were in the *Daily News*, the *New York Post*, *New York Times*, *Guitar Magazine*, *US Magazine*. That's how we got on the show. So we were there, and he said, "Benjy, do you guys have children?" And I said, "Yeah, Manudo, and they're making a lot of money." And the crowd was laughing. But they loved that about us. We were a very charming band, you know what I mean. And it was fantastic. What a show when we played there. Everybody's looking at us, they're clapping, standing ovation! Regis said, "Where did you guys learn to play like that?" And there was a professor and his wife, from

Columbia University, they taught music, they looked at us, they were old people, "Where did you get those voices? Because now, I'm listening to you do those Beatles songs and I now I understand what you're saying. I couldn't understand what The Beatles said. But I understand the way you guys are saying it." So they found that Amazing.

This was 1982/'83, between that time. One time, we were interviewing with Dinah Shore, right in front of the Lincoln Center. And every time I'd talk to her, my nose would start bleeding. And she started to laugh. It was crazy. So we received good press when we were Street the Beat. And we played many private parties for lots of celebrities. We played for The Rolling Stones and The Village People. You know the Indian guy in The Village People? My brother Victor said, "See, Benjy, he's half Puerto-Rican." I said, "No, he isn't." And I went up to him and he said he is, his mother is Cherokee. So we played there. We played for The Doors, without Morrison, he had already died. The remaining members of The Doors, they invited us to Urbana. You know, where the ball drops on 42nd Street? We were up there. That's an Indian restaurant. They had us playing in a private party. Aretha Franklin, her back-up singers. Diana Ross. We're singing right across the street from Lincoln Center. She's walking this way, and out of my peripheral vision, I see a dress, a real shiny dress. She's very thin. She walks up to me, she puts $100 in my pocket. She says, "Man, you guys are good!" We met Grandpa from the television show "The Munsters." We met Martin Sheen. We met Brooke Shields. We met a lot of important people back in the days.

We played for this millionaire, Rick Alexander. He lived in the Dakota Hotel, where John Lennon was killed. He said, "How would you guys like to play the Dakota?" We said, "Oh, man, that would be cool!" So we played for him three times. Three times! He's a millionaire. So we're looking at his apartment saying, "Man, this place is NICE!" I asked him, "Rick, how much do you pay rent here?" He said, "You wouldn't wanna know."

When we played private parties our manager would tell them, "If you're going to hire us electric, it's gonna cost you more money. If you want something compatible, something that's easy, that won't be too loud in the apartment, we'll bring the custom-made drums." And that's what they wanted to hear anyway. You know why? The voices! They were raw. You could hear all of the harmony. The electric drowns things out.

We had a great manager at the time. Peter Halpern. He loved, loved, loved the band so much.

•••

After the Ghetto Brothers was over, my brother Victor tried several times to quit his dope habit. Finally, many years later, he gets into a methadone program on Arthur Avenue, in the Bronx. It was way after the gang era and the organization had finished. This was when he contracted AIDS.

When he was taking the methadone, he wasn't using dope. He wanted to get out of it. But he told me, "Benjy, it's hard." "Why, Victor?" "Because I've been doing this so long. It's been part of me. So, in order for me to talk at your level, I have to be high. My greatest fear is to stop using dope." That really hurt me, but I had to understand where he came from. You know, so I said, "O.K., Victor, I understand." Not too long after that, Victor died. And when I lost my brother, it was another world. First my father, now my brother, who I also learned a lot from and who I looked up to, was gone.

•••

In 1991, I was diagnosed with diabetes. I was scared 'cause I thought I sat on a toilet and I caught AIDS. Remember, people didn't know, and the ignorance was big back then. And I cried and I cried. I said to Wanda, "I can't do nothing with you. 'Cause I don't want you to get sick." I was losing weight, I was 260 pounds, and I went down to like 170, maybe less. I was losing weight, my teeth were coming out. People were looking at me, "Yo, Benjy, what happened to you?" I was like, "I'm sick, man, I don't know what's going on." Wanda took me to the hospital. Wanda said, "You'll be all right." They checked my blood, the following day, they called me in for emergency. My blood count was 800. So that's it, that's what they diagnosed me for, diabetes. From then on, they gave me pills and the needle. And that's why my kidneys got messed up big time.

But I learned to cope with diabetes. And the music still never stopped. Years after Street the Beat, I started the Ghetto Brothers band again. This time with my brother and nephew in the line up.

Then, there was another painful day for me. One day, I went to the studio. My son, John, used to take care of my nephew's sons. John was 24. My nephew said, "John, take care of my children. I'll pay you. 'Cause we gotta go to the studio." John said, "O.K." That same night we went to the studio, we just walked in, I get a phone call. Tánto, my nephew, calls. He said, "Put Benjy on the phone." I get the phone, I said, "Yeah, what's happening?" "Yo, Benjy. Your son fell on the floor; he couldn't breathe." As soon as he said that, now I know. Wanda had told him, "Take the needle with you." You know that special needle? He had asthma. It would open up his lungs. He didn't want to take it. You know how mothers are with the intuition, "John, you don't look good. Please don't go." He said, "Mommy, everything's gonna be O.K. I'll be all right." John had attacks, but he knew how to get out of it.

But soon as I heard that: *fell on the floor*, my brother Robert looked at me; and a tear started to fall from my eye. A big tear came out. I said, "My son died." I called Wanda, "Wanda, go to Tánto's house. I think something's happening with John." She didn't go to the apartment, the ambulance had already picked John up. They took him to Lincoln Hospital. When they told me to come into the room at Lincoln Hospital, I walked inside of the room and saw his body just laying there. I cried like a child. And I held his feet. I said, "Wanda, they're going to put my son in the grave, in the cold, cold grave. I don't want him there. I want him cremated. I want him to stay with me." She said, "O.K." We agreed. It didn't hit Wanda until we got home. Then she let out this scream, like a cat.

So I had him home with me. Everywhere I go, he stays with me. 'Cause that was my torment. To know that my son is out there in the grave, cold? I couldn't bare it.

∙ ∙ ∙

When I look back on everything, the gang era, the Ghetto Brothers gang and our transition, and I think about how much difference the Ghetto Brothers actually made, I look at it like World War II, like we're coming from a big battle, a final, decisive battle, that was the start of the end of the gang wars in the Bronx. I lived through a LOT! I grew into a man amidst some of the worst conditions any human should ever have to go through. Crime, murder, poverty, the city forgetting about us, ignoring an entire community. Buildings burning. Drugs everywhere. It was a hopeless situation, but I never lost hope. I lost my way at different times along the way. But I have no mistakes to complain about. I have no regrets. I did my duty. I wasn't perfect, but I cared for the people. And I put my life on the line to try to get change. The Peace Meeting was accomplished and good things came out of that. So I did my part.

I remember this time my little boy, Joshua, my very first son, from MayLin. When he was a little boy, he asked me, "Papi, what have you done for people?" He was just a little boy when he asked me that. I said, "I've done a lot for this society. I've saved the lives of thousands of people." And I told him the whole story. And he just stood there. Then he said, "Weren't you scared?" I told him, "Of course, 'cause I could've been killed." Then he says to me, "Wow, Pa, that sounds like a comic book." Yeah. But it was real.

Photo Album

Benjy "Yellow Benjy" Melendez (ca. 1971)

L to R: Members of the Ghetto Brothers, Roman Kings, and Ghetto Brothers

L to R: Taino Louis (Ghetto Brothers), Satch (Savage Skulls), Chino (Turbins), and Benjy (Ghetto Brothers)

L to R: Angel Vasquez, Benjy, Victor, David Silva, Robert, and Charlie (ca. 1971)

L to R: Charlie and Benjy (ca. 1972)

L to R: Benjy and Tony Batten on television show "51st State" (1972)

Benjy on television show "51st State" (1972)

L to R: Colors of South Bronx street gangs — Bronx Aliens, Tomahawks, Dirty Dozen, Black Spades, Bachelors, and Seven Immortals

L to R: Benjy and Victor (ca. 1972)

Benjy performing with the Ghetto Brothers band (ca. 1972)

"Bull" Bristo (ca. 1972)

Franky Valentine (ca. 1972)

Mike (ca. 1972)

Victor Melendez (ca. 1972)

Robert Melendez (ca. 1972)

Benjy (ca. 1972)

David Silva (ca. 1972)

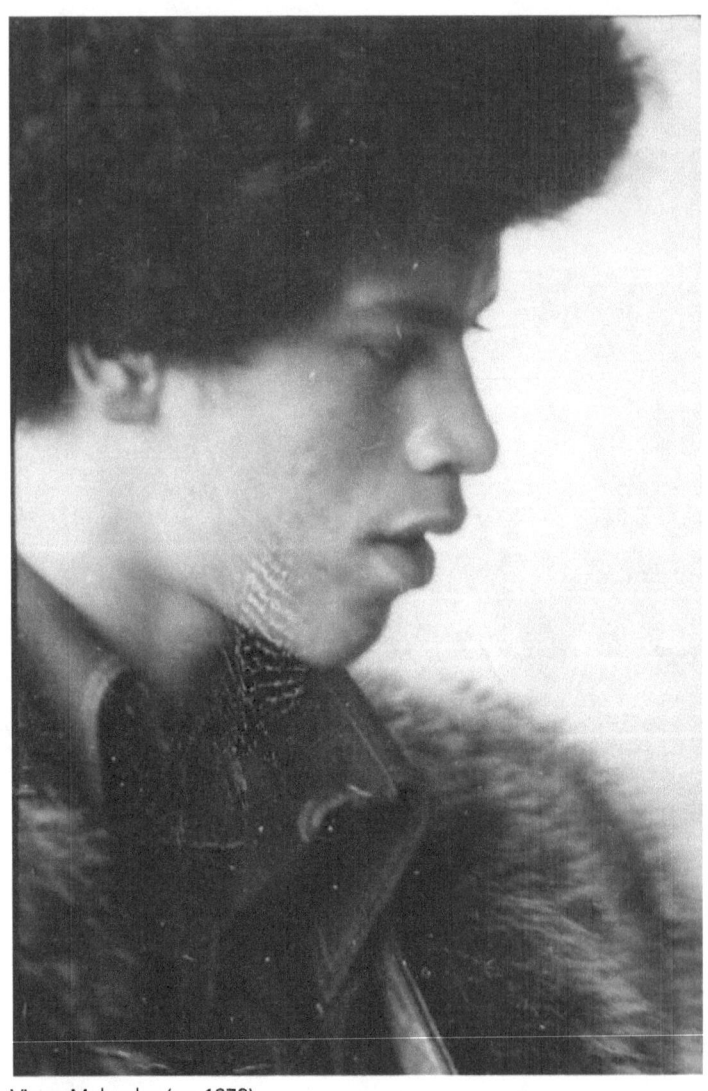
Victor Melendez (ca. 1972)

Franky Valentine (ca. 1972)

Power Fuerza album cover, front

Ghetto Brothers

SLP 2008

SIDE A
1 — GIRL FROM THE MOUNTAIN
  (FELIX TOLLINCHI)
2 — THERE IS SOMETHING IN MY HEART
  (BENNY MELENDEZ)
3 — GOT THIS HAPPY FEELING
  (BENNY MELENDEZ)
4 — MASTICA, CHUPA Y JALA
  (VICTOR MELENDEZ)

SIDE B
1 — YOU SAY THAT YOU'RE MY FRIEND
  (BENNY MELENDEZ)
2 — VIVA PUERTO RICO LIBRE
  (BENNY MELENDEZ)
3 — I SAW A TEAR
  (VICTOR MELENDEZ)
4 — GHETTO BROTHERS POWER
  (VICTOR MELENDEZ)

PERSONNEL
Lead Guitar: DAVID SILVA
Rythm Guitar: ROBERT MELENDEZ
Bass: VICTOR MELENDEZ
Lead Vocal: BENNY MELENDEZ
Congas: CHIQUI CONCEPCION
Drums: LUIS BRISTO
Timbales: FRANKY VALENTIN
Bongos: ANGELO GARCIA

CREDITS
Production: BOBBY MARIN
Studio: PINETONE
Photography: GARY MASON
Cover Design: ANGELO VELAZQUEZ

This album contains a message; a message to the world, from the Ghetto Brothers. The Ghetto Brothers, a community organization dedicated to bridging the ever-increasing gap that exists between society and minority groups, believe music to be the common language of the world. Through music, they are able to inform society of the plight of the 'little people' in their quest for recognition. Therefore, the music of the Ghetto Brothers serves as a way of communication.

If the Ghetto Brothers' dream comes true, the world will learn that the 'little people' wish to be acknowledged, wish to be properly educated in order for them to pass on their knowledge to their children and proudly inform them about their heritage and culture, and be a functioning part of the growth of America. If the Ghetto Brothers' dream comes true, the 'little people' will be 'little people' no more, and make their own mark in this world. Listen to the Ghetto Brothers....... and take heed.

Power Fuerza album cover, back

Benjy (ca. 1972)

L to R: Charlie, bystander, and Benjy (ca. 1972)

Peacemaker Beaten, Slain In Gang Fight

By EDWARD KIRKMAN and JOHN MURPHY

A 25-year-old youth worker who specialized in the risky role of peacemaker among warring gangs in the South Bronx was struck down and killed by a pipe-wielding gang member yesterday as he sought to mediate a feud, police said.

The incident began, acquaintances of slain Cornell Benjamin said, when a quarrel erupted among youths over a handball game at the John Dwyer Junior High School, 1010 Stebbins Ave., near 165th St., Bronx.

One of the handball players, Hermino Madera, 15, was attacked there at about 1 p.m., police said, by a number of members of two gangs, the Black Spades and the Seven Immortals, wielding lead pipes.

Third Faction Intrudes

School officials rescued Madera, who was taken to Lincoln Hospital in reportedly fair condition.

Meanwhile, the slum grapevine swiftly brought news of the attack to the storefront headquarters of the Ghetto Brothers, a neighborhood youth group sponsored by the city Youth Services Agency, at 881 E. 162d St. The grapevine also brought some 50 other gang members to the scene, keen for trouble.

Lei Melendez, an ex-marine and president of the Ghetto Brothers, said he heard the news with Benjamin as they sat in the storefront headquarters.

Teeners Clash Again

Melendez, who said Benjamin was an eager "expert" at mediating gang wars, remained in the office as Benjamin left to try to calm the situation.

Minutes later, Benjamin, known to neighborhood youths as "Black Benjie," appeared at 165th St. and Rogers Pl. near the school accompanied by a white youth.

Police said that by this time, young members of the Black Spades and the Seven Immortals—many only 13 or 14 years old—who had joined to beat Madera, were now angrily confronting one another.

Dead on Arrival

Benjamin, police said, tried to talk peace to the youths but the youth with him apparently panicked, took off his belt and lashed at several youths before running away.

A number of the gang members then jumped Benjamin, and knocked him to the ground, police said. One youth battered him with a pipe.

Police summoned to the scene took Benjamin to Lincoln Hospi-

(Continued on page 81, col. 3)

'Peacemaker' Gives His Life

(Continued from page 3)

tal, where he was pronounced dead.

Some time later, police seized George Peterson, 18, of 1240 Franklin Ave., Bronx, at Intervale and Westchester Aves. They booked him on a homicide charge in Benjamin's death.

Dwyer's Principal Morton Weinberger said that area gangs had sparked trouble in the school recently. He said his faculty was understrength and police protection inadequate. He blamed budget cuts for the understaffing.

Told His Story on TV

Benjamin, described as a former drug addict devoted to shaping up errant kids in the South Bronx, appeared on the Channel 13 TV program "Free Time" with other Ghetto Brothers a month ago.

The group rapped on slum street life, the frustrations of South Bronx youth and the shadow of drug addiction overlying their lives.

The Ghetto Brothers are reported to be chiefly Puerto Rican but with a scattering of black and a few whites.

Despite the activities of the Ghetto Brothers as mediators, the Black Spades and Seven Immortals have reportedly turned the area around Dwyer into a "no man's land" in a war over "turf," reminiscent of similar bloody conflict among the numerous "rumbling" youth gangs of the late 1940s and '50s.

Weinberger, speaking of yesterday's incident, said: "This was bound to come."

Dollar Dives

The value of the United States dollar dropped to record lows on foreign exchange markets around the world yesterday in a reaction to reports that the U.S., in a policy turnaround, is willing to consider devaluation of the dollar. See story p. 56.

Cornell "Black Benjie" Benjamin (1971)

Violence Won't Bring Benjie Back, Says Youth Leader

By EMILE MILNE

Leaders of the Ghetto Brothers, a South Bronx youth gang, have vowed they will try to prevent more gang violence over the slaying of one of their members earlier this week.

"All the clubs are waiting for one word—fire—but I'm not going to say fire, because that won't bring Benjie back." Benjamin Melendez, 17, president of the Ghetto Brothers said.

Cornell Benjamin, 25, (also known as Black Benjie), vice president of the Ghetto Brothers, was beaten to death Thursday when he tried to intervene as a peacemaker between two other gangs, the Black Spades and Seven Immortals, who had squared off for a fight.

George Peterson, 18, of 1240 Franklin Av., a member of the Black Spades, was seized on the street later that night and charged with homicide.

The death of Benjamin, who was well-known and liked in the area as a peacemaker, has spurred widespread fears of a recurrence of mass gang violence that racked the city in the 1950s.

Extra Cops Assigned

The Police Dept., in an effort to ease what it calls a "tense" situation in the blighted South Bronx neighborhood, has called additional men, including members of the Tactical Patrol Force, into the area to provide beefed-up patrols.

A police spokesman said, however, there was little fear of renewed gang warfare, at least until "police protection is slackened."

Gang violence resulted in at least one other homicide in the South Bronx this year, when a 54-year-old man was shot and beaten to death last spring, according to police. There have been numerous gang-related assaults police said.

Benjamin, a reformed drug addict, lived with his widowed mother, a social worker, Mrs. Gwendolyn Benjamin, in a city housing project at 535 Jackson Av. He had four sisters and two brothers.

He gained the respect and admiration of the Ghetto Brothers after joining them more than a year ago, while trying to transform a "street gang" into a "political force." Less than a month ago he persuaded the "Brothers" members to discard their "colors"—a patch worn to distinguish one gang from another.

Under his leadership and that of other community activists, the gang has participated in food and clothing drives, the formation of a soul band and had generally stayed clear of narcotics.

"He made it turn into a brotherhood," a Ghetto Brothers member said. "If he had a piece of bread everybody shared it. All the cops wanted to see was Puerto Ricans and blacks fighting each other. So Benjie got hip to that and tried to get us together."

The Ghetto Brothers, who have recently received widespread attention because of their musical ability and attempts at creating a better "gang image," last month convened a meeting of most of the South Bronx leadership in Central Park to sign a "peace treaty."

That treaty, some members feel, has been broken. "The Savage Nomads, the Savage Sculls, Turbans, Roman Kings, Bachelors, all the clubs were there," said one Ghetto Brothers member. "The Black Spades and the Seven Immortals were the only ones that broke the treaty."

John Gay, training coordinator at the Trinity Av. Block Assn., who has been involved in counseling South Bronx youths, said he expected "feelings are going to run high for retaliation," but that he hoped gang members would "let the law deal with it."

He also cautioned that police need "not turn the community into an armed camp" but rather make an effort to "come in here and understand what is going on by walking and talking to the people who live here."

To All Brothers and Sisters;

We realize that we are all brothers living in the same neighborhoods and having the same problems. We also realize that fighting among ourselves will not solve our common problems. If we are to build up our community to be better place for our families and ourselves we must work together. We who have signed this treaty pledge peace and unity for all. All of us who have signed this peace will be known from now on as The Family.

The terms fo the Peace are as follows:

1. All groups are to respect each other – cliques individual members and their women. Each member clique of the Family will be able to wear their colors in other member cliques' turf without being bothered. They are to remember in whose turf they are and respect that turf as if it were their own.

2. If any clique has a gripe against another clique the presidents of each are to meet together to talk it out.
If one member of a clique has a beef with a member of another clique, the two are to talk it over. If that does not solve it then they will both fight it out between themselves, after that it is considered finished.
If there is any rumors about cliques going down on each other the leaders of each of these groups shall meet to talk it out.

3. For those cliques outside of the Peace Treaty – the presidents of the Family will meet with the clique to explain the terms of the Peace. The clique will given the opportunity to–
    a. join
    b. disband
    c. be disbanded.

4. The presidents of the Family will meet from time to time to discuss concerns of the groups.

This is the Peace we pledge to keep.

PEACE BETWEEN ALL GANGS AND A POWERFUL UNITY

1. Power
2. The Ghetto Brothers
3. The Black Pearls
4. The Evil Serpent's
5. Mafestic Warlocks
6. Roman Kings
7. Renegades
8. The Slics
9. United Lords
10. Young Sinners
11. Black Ivory
12. Mongols
13. Savage Nomads
14. Seven Immortals
15. The Black Cats INC.
16. The Shapes of Black
17. The Blue Imperalils
18. The Deserters
19. The Brothers & Sisters
20. Latin Aces
21. Born to Raise Hell
22. Spanish Daggers
23. Savage Skulls
24. Latin Kings
25. Royal Swords
26. Immortals New York
27. The Young Saigons
28. The Black Spades
29. 1# The Turbans
30. 4# The Turbans
31. 5# The Turbans
32. Dominican Lions
33. Dirty Dozen
34. Fox St. Assoc.
35. Spanish Skulls
36. Javeline
37. Mac. 7 Roun
38. Liberated Panthers
39. 1 Peace Makers
40. 2 Peace Makers
41. Bachelors
42. Flaming Lords

L to R: Benjy and Charlie — Benjy given karate lessons (ca. 1971)

I came from were alive, I came breathing better, and better, so I could do it that is concentrated in that little dreams.

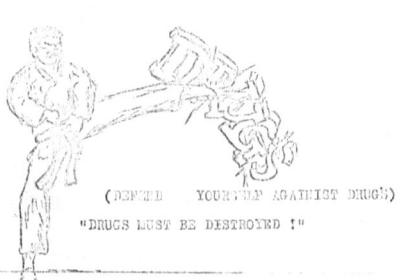

(DEFEND YOURSELF AGAINST DRUGS)
"DRUGS MUST BE DESTROYED!"

(IT'S KILL OR BE KILLED)

BLACK POWER, WHITE POWER,
AND PUERTO RICAN POWER,
EVEN KARATE POWER!

(BUT NO DOPE POWER)

L to R: Vick Miles and Benjy (interview, ca. 1976)

L to R: David Silva, Benjy, Victor, Regis Philbin, Robert Melendez, and Manny Cortez. ("The Morning Show," ca. 1985)

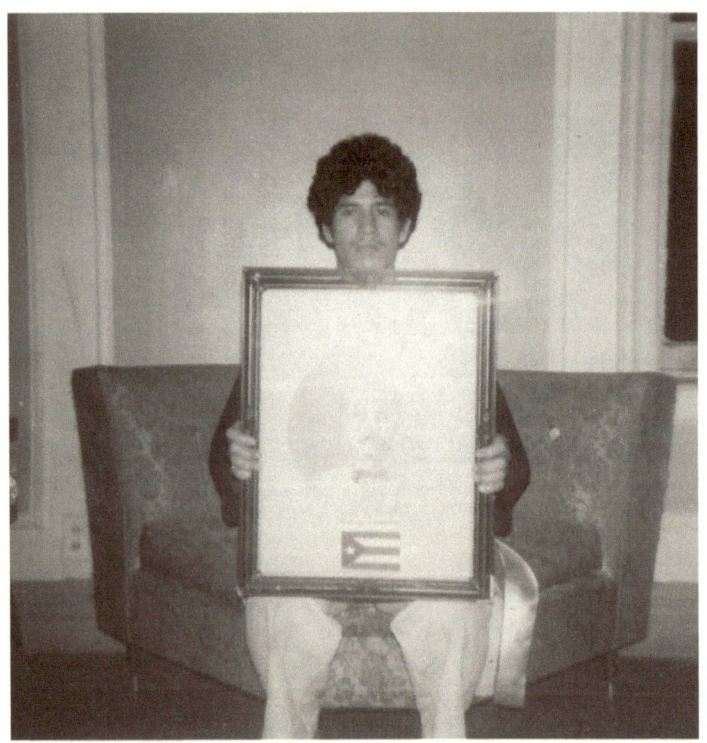
Benjy Melendez holding photo of Pedro Albizu Campos (ca. 1972)

Benjy 'Yellow Benjy" Melendez
(2015)

Acknowledgments

Benjy Melendez acknowledges:

I'd like to thank Said (Amir Said) for making this book happen, and for his kindness, knowledge, and support. Rita Fecher, my friend, who, along wiht Henry Chalfant, directed the film *Flyin' Cut Sleeves*. Henry Chalfant, who has been a good friend to me, and who has always looked out for me. Joey Conzo. My brothers Victor, Robert, and Bobby. David Silva. Joe Schloss. Zev and Avi. And my wife, Wanda, who has been with me through thick and thin. All with much love.

—Yellow Benjy

Amir Said acknowledges:

Amir Ali Said, my son, best friend, and Superchamp co-founder — Thank you for your friendship, knowledge, courage, and curiosity. Remember, all the answers are in three places: Q, S, and YT.

Qamar, my son's mother — Your love, belief, and support through the years has meant, and will always mean, something incredibly special to me. Thank you.

Benjy, thank you for entrusting your life's story to me. You are an incredibly kind, warm, generous, and genuine individual, one with many shining life-moments that have helped shaped New York City and beyond. Mariella Gross, thank you for your unwavering commitment and understanding. Silvana, you are a wonderful person, you've been a tremendous source of support, helping me in ways you can not imagine — Thank you for listening, talking, and sharing; every artist should be so fortunate to have someone like you.

—Said

About the Authors

Benjy Melendez is a community leader, social activist, and musician. He was the founder and leader of the Ghetto Brothers street grang, one of the biggest, most notorious and influential street gangs in New York City history. He was also the co-founder and lead singer of the Ghettos Brothers band, who's lone album, *Power Fuerza*, is still one of the most sought after records among collectors everywhere. Benjy lives in New York with his wife, Wanda, and continues to play music with his band The Ghetto Brothers, which is a reimagined line up of the original Ghetto Brothers band.

Amir Said is an author, musician, and publisher from Brooklyn, New York. He's written a number of books including *The BeatTips Manual*, *The Art of Sampling*, *Medium Speed in the City Called Paris (Poetry)*, and *The Truth About New York*. His new books, *Feed the Meter* (a novel), and *The Bungalow Bar* (a novel) will be published in 2018.

www.ingramcontent.com/pod-product-compliance
Lightning Source LLC
Chambersburg PA
CBHW030436300426
44112CB00009B/1025